11/29/2013

Happy Birthday, Jan!

May Nikki entertain you
inspire you throughout the
year ... Love,
Mary & Pete

Chasing Utopia

ALSO BY NIKKI GIOVANNI

Chasing Utopia

NIKKI GIOVANNI

A Hybrid

WILLIAM MORROW
An Imprint of HarperCollins*Publishers*

HarperCollins books may be purchased for educational, business, or sales promotional use. For information please e-mail the: Special Markets Department at SPsales@harpercollins.com.

FIRST EDITION

Library of Congress Cataloging-in-Publication Data has been applied for.

ISBN 978-0-688-15697-8

13   14   15   16   17   RRD   10   9   8   7   6   5   4   3   2   1

For Aunt Agnes and Sister Althea,
my two oldest friends on Earth

For the gypsy in my soul

CONTENTS

Chasing Utopia

So here is the actual story. I was bored. Well, not bored because I had the privilege of interviewing Mae Jemison, the first Black woman in space, who said she pursued a degree in physics and also became a medical doctor to keep her mind occupied. Mae's IQ must be nine hundred and fifty-five or thereabouts. I asked: "How do you keep from being bored?" And she replied: "A friend of my father's once told me 'If you're bored you're not paying attention.'"

So I said to myself: "Beer."

We are foodies, my family and I. My grandmother was an extraordinary cook. Her miniature Parker House rolls have been known to float the roof off a flooded house in hurricane season. Grandpapa made pineapple ice cream so rich and creamy with those surprising chunks that burst with citrusy flavor. My sister made Spring Rolls so perfectly the Chinese complained to the State Department and my aunt fries chicken just short of burning that has been known to make the Colonel denounce his own KFC. Mommy is the best bean cooker in this world or the next and I do a pretty swell pot roast. We are, in other words, dangerous when it comes to food. But I'm a wine drinker. My sister was a wine drinker also. Red, of course. One aunt married a minister so they ate their wine instead of drinking it. That left Mommy and my middle aunt, Ann, as the beer drinkers.

Mommy also liked Pig Feet. Boiled. Not Pickled.

I was sad when Mommy died. Then six weeks later Gary died. Then my aunt Ann. I tried to find a way to bring them back.

Beer.

Mommy drank Miller Genuine Draft. Ann drank Bud Light. Not for me. If it was going to be Beer I needed to learn something.

Going through books I came across Utopia. Sam Adams. The #1 Beer in the World. Having always been a fan of *start at the top* I called my local beer store. "I'd like to order a Utopia, please." Thinking this would be easy. "No Way," Keith said. "We never get that!" O.K. I called Bounty Hunter. They have everything. I bought my Justice Series: Blind Justice, Frontier Justice, Poetic Justice. Great red wines. "No, ma'am, we don't sell beer." In Canada they sell Utopia as a Special Brew because the alcohol content is so high but it's still a beer.

But here is the happy part. I am a poet. I occasionally get invited to speak at Important Government Agencies. I was thrilled. Sure, someone will say why would you, a poet, a rebel, you who hate the TSA and think Railroads should make a big comeback, you who think modern wars are stupid and unworthy . . . why would you speak for an Important Government Agency? Well for one thing I am an American. So government, whether I like it or not, R Me. For another thing I know they have the world's best computers. I was charming; I was funny. I was very nice and a good citizen. I wanted an illegal favor.

"Please, Sir," said I, "can you find Utopia?" "Of course, Little Lady," said the Director. "It's in your heart and mind." He smiled a lovely smile and patted me on my shoulder. Not wanting to appear to correct him I smiled the smile of the defeated. And waited for him to leave. I asked his assistant. "I think," he pontificated, "it is in your soul. Search deep and you will find it." I knew I needed someone of color. Finally an older man, gray hair cut short, came by. "Please excuse me," I said, "I'm trying to find Utopia. Can you help?" "Why sure," he said, "as soon as I can find a safe computer." We moved into another room and he made me stand way away from him so that I could not see the computer screen. He pulled up a website. "Here you go." And he was right. "I can't buy it as it's against the rules but get someone else to go to this site. I hear it's a great beer. At $350 a pint it ought to be."

And now that I've found Utopia I am at peace . . . drinking the Jazz Series from Dogfish brewery: Brother Thelonious, Bitches Brew, Hellhound on My Ale. I have Utopia and if I were Egyptian I would be buried with it. I use it to start conversations and make friends. It is not for Mortals. Or Americans. Utopia is for Poets . . . or the Gods.

A SHORT ESSAY NOT ON WHY I DON'T ASK PERSONAL QUESTIONS BUT A BALANCING SHARING ON WHEN I FIRST DID

I went to the memory bank to see when it was that I last asked a personal question since we were talking and I said to you: *I don't.* When it got to be more than twenty years back I began to feel the journey wasn't worth it but then I said: *Oh, put ten more years in.* I still couldn't come up with a question. The last person I asked a personal question of, I think, is Sister Althea and I wanted to know why she became a nun. I must have been twelve or thirteen years old. Thank goodness she took it in the love it was given or I guess in this case Asked.

So I thought since I had asked a personal question of you, mainly: *What were you like at 17?* I thought I should answer it about myself.

I asked because my own journey begins not actually at 17 but events that would make 17 a mountain began to be put in place. My aunt Ann lived in Philadelphia and my grandfather wanted to go visit her. I was living with Grandmother and Grandpapa in Knoxville and was in school at Austin High. There are still memories I need to mine to see the how and why but I knew I couldn't live with my parents and my grandparents were kind enough to take me in. I think now the reason I went to Philadelphia with Grandpapa and not Grandmother is that we probably could only afford two tickets. I wasn't thinking about that then or maybe Grandmother had meetings (she was a committed club woman: Garden, Book, Deaconess, Bridge, NAACP among others). Grandmother was very popular so she may have had commitments. At any rate Grandpapa and I took the train to Philly. It was a day trip, change in DC and we were there that night. I learned the subway system the hard way: I got on and rode to Center City. I walked to the Liberty Bell and purchased a little copy for my mother which sits still on my dresser. I was very proud of myself because I am mostly adventurous in my head. I had lunch at the Reading Market and went back home by subway. I was thrilled that I could do it.

A day or so later we received a call from Grandmother. She said I needed to come back to Knoxville because she had talked with Mme. Stokes, the French teacher, who told her there was a test I should take. The Ford Foundation had a program called Early Entrant to College. You take a test, do well, and you go off to college. Grandmother was always thrilled when any of us did well so she thought I should come home and take the test. That would have meant Grandpapa would have to cut short his trip which didn't seem right. Uncle Haynes took me to the train station and gave me directions about changing in DC. I learned later he also asked the Pullman Porters to look out for me.

The first book I ever bought for myself was a biography of Clarence Darrow, *Attorney for the Damned,* but I doubt I was reading anything so useful. Most likely something trashy, since I've always been a fan of trashy heroes. I bought a small box of chocolate chip cookies and sat down. One of my good things is I can actually sit still for interminable lengths of time. I didn't do much between Philly and DC but be a bit nervous about making my connection.

After DC it was on to Knoxville. I no longer had to worry so I opened my book and my chocolate chip cookies. Two young white soldiers started to talk about me: *She has those cookies; I wonder if she'll give us one.* I remember looking at them. They were as young as I was or so they seemed. I said: *Do you want a cookie?* And they laughed. They meant me no harm. They were, I later realized, flirting with me. I didn't understand it then because I didn't know that I was pretty. I was 16.

I passed the test. Never graduated from high school. Went to Fisk. Got kicked out. Failed. Then learned failure is as important as success. I still don't ask many questions. But I do try to pay attention.

If a lemon
Kissed a beet
Is it sour
Or is it sweet

If a bear
Gives
A hug
Will it turn
Into a rug

And then there's me
And there is you
I do sometimes wonder
What will we do

I loved before
I understood;
Love is a skill

I loved my Mother's cool hands
On my forehead

I loved the safety
Of her arms
I trusted
Before I understood
The word

Mommy would say
When I had fallen:
"Come here, Nikki,
and I'll pick you up"

and I would wipe my eyes
push myself off my fat bottom
and tottle over to her
for my reward:
a kiss and a "That's my Big Girl!"

I am still a sucker
For that one

But I grew up
And learned
Trust and love
Are crafts we practice
Are wheels
We balance
Our lives on

Are BICYCLES
We ride
Through *challenges and changes*

To **escape** and **ecstasy**

My grandfather was twenty years older than my grandmother so he was an old man when we, the grandchildren, met him. He didn't seem all that old and he was a very patient man but he didn't hang out and laugh with us the way Grandmother did. We cooked with Grandmother and did chores. Grandpapa attended to the grocery chores and cut the grass. He was also a Deacon at our church, Mt. Zion Baptist Church. He seemed formidable.

For whatever the reason he liked me. He liked my younger cousin, Terry, also calling him Terry the Brick. He would on his deathbed charge Terry with "take care of the women." Which Terry has done.

I am the only grandchild to live with them. During the Age of Segregation I went back to Knoxville, the place of my birth, and lived with my grandparents and attended Austin High School.

But before all that we four, my older sister, Gary, and Terry and his older brother, William, spent summers in Knoxville. The two boys, being boys, were up early, breakfasted, and off to the playground or the park or swimming or whatever it is boys do until lunch when they are famished, then off again. My sister liked to cook so she and Grandmother would huddle in the kitchen baking wonderful things. Me . . . I was set adrift. I would, some days, ask Grandmother if I could go to the library which was at the top of our street, Mulvaney. I always enjoyed dusting, it was my chore at home, so some days I would dust then read something from Grandmother's library. Grandmother wanted to teach me to play the piano but I was too dumb to know that one day I would wish she had.

I guess Grandpapa noticed that I was by myself a lot.

He would call me over to read an Aesop Fable or to teach me a Latin verb. I guess he wanted to make me feel needed or interesting or something. In the evenings before there was so much neon that the stars were blotted out, he would invite me to walk with him and he would point out the stars to me, guiding me on a journey through the Underground Railroad. He was a good storyteller and a great teacher. But I was always disturbed by a couple of the Aesop Fables. I didn't like the way the "Mice in Council" ended. It seemed someone should be brave enough and courageous enough to bell that cat even if a supreme sacrifice had to be made. What little bit of history I was learning showed there is always a hero or heroine in the case of Jeanne d'Arc or Harriet Tubman who risked it all for freedom and justice. As I was older I added Rosa Parks to that list and Daisy Bates. I was particularly angry about "The Grasshopper and the Ants."

Grandpapa was always on the side of the Ants. He thought the Grasshopper should have saved up for a "rainy day." I thought the Grasshopper was being abused by the Ants, though I did not have *abuse* in my vocabulary then.

We were Baptist, though I'm sure other Protestants do the same thing. Every Sunday, we youngsters went to church. We had a dime apiece: a nickel for Sunday School, a nickel for ice cream, since in those days you could buy an ice-cream cone for a nickel. We would all walk together to Carter-Roberts Drug Store for our ice cream but we had to be back to church on time.

After church we would go home; change clothes; then take a plate of dinner to the "sick and shut-in." There was no variation with this. Dinner in the South on Sunday is early because we were probably going either back to church or to visit another church in the evening. It was the right thing to do. I couldn't understand when we read "The Grasshopper and the Ants" how the Ants could send the poor Grasshopper out into the cold to freeze to death. Grandpapa and I argued about that one a lot. I, of course, always lost.

Time, however, was on my side. I grew up to become a writer which let me think and think and think again about issues. And in the back of my mind there were these Ants and this Grasshopper. I was still unhappy about the justification of taking advantage of the Grasshopper's better nature. Then an opportunity came to me to write about it and I seized that moment.

The Grasshopper, like Sisyphus, was an artist. We, Grandpapa and I, had argued about Sisyphus, too. He was not, in my opinion, being punished for bringing fire but rather, like all Artists, challenged to create, yet again. The rock was not there to torment him but rather to remind him he had work yet to do. The Grasshopper made music. And where would we be without music?

There is a reason when we step into an elevator there is music playing. You are about to get into a box which will rise higher than you can jump. In order to soothe you and make you think everything is all right we play music. The same with an airplane. Your dentist tells you to bring your favorite CDs to play while he drills your nerves. And we all know when we are afraid we "whistle a happy tune." Music is the first and, I believe, most essential tool in combating the unknown.

I could have had the Grasshopper go in to destroy the Ants but that would have been unintelligent. The Grasshopper did the American thing: He sued. For R-E-S-P-E-C-T. Of course, respect might come later but half the harvest would be primary. "Am I not worthy of my bread?" the Plaintiff, the Grasshopper, asked.

And the Ants tried to respond by asking for a Contract. But isn't a Contract the services we accept as much as the services we ask for? Aren't the great ideas of this nation based on the Mayflower Compact, an agreement of mutual assistance not just on who can beat whom out of what? Where is the justice if we only follow the letter instead of the spirit of the law? Young people need to know the law is our shield, our Gladiator, our protection. Right makes Might and not the other way around.

The Grasshopper prevails because he put his faith in the twelve good people who impartially heard his story. The Ants needed to learn they were helped with the art and soul the Grasshopper offered. They needed to learn to share.

And they all lived happily ever after because the law said it is good and right to be fair to everyone. Greed is un-American. Thievery is un-American. It is good to recognize and understand that we all benefit from paying our fair share of taxes, treating our friends and colleagues fairly.

Grandpapa and Aesop were wrong. The Grasshopper did contribute. Where would we be without the imagination that encounters with art and artists bring? We'd be little Ants working day and night selfishly hoarding the bounty nature provides with no joy in the benefits of our work. We can . . . and we should . . . do better than that.

Chocolate cookies
Chocolate cakes
Chocolate fudge
Chocolate lakes
Chocolate kisses
Chocolate hugs
Two little chocolate girls
In a chocolate rug

No one can find us
We're all alone
Two little chocolate girls
Running from home

Chocolate chickies
Chocolate bunnies
Chocolate smiles
From chocolate mommies
Chocolate rabbits
Chocolate snakes
Two little chocolate girls
Wide awake

What an adventure
My, what fun
My sister and me
Still on the run
Still on the run
My sister and me
Still
On the run

i used to watch
my mother cook
she would invariably sigh
a little sigh then light
a cigarette

since no one smokes
anymore Beans
have not tasted as good

i have her sigh
and stacks of spices

"This one is cardamom
It comes from Southeast Asia"
"This one is nutmeg
the defense of this spice by a Brit was so fierce
the world court heard the case and the Dutch
gave up Manhattan Island for the little island
in the Indian Ocean that grew nutmegs"
and cloves . . . stick them in an orange for a
Christmas present
or a ham to make
a design

cooking with Mommy was
Geography "These pansies you can eat"
"These mushrooms will
kill you" (should we put them in your father's
eggs? she'd laugh
and say)

the green things
rosemary thyme tarragon cilantro

the fennel we grew brought mean
yellow jackets so
we get it at Kroger's

"The trick to a great
Ham
is a song" she'd say
And we would sing loud and lustily
She harmonizing with me but me
Unable to carry a straight melody

Now it is ready

cold water almost to the top
fennel allspice pepper pods of all colors
       No Salt—it's a rule
green spices till it
looks right then
cinnamon on the uncovered top
low heat until boiling
(about 2 hours)
let cool 15 minutes
pour off water then
let cool on your platter

I make my Ham the way
my mother made hers
with lots of talk and love and laughter

Corn bread muffins
A streak of lean
Mustard greens simmering
On Grandmother's stove
Boiled ham
Fresh churned butter
Grandpapa reading the comics to Grandmother
And me
While we cook
I set the table
With the everyday dishes
They both like ice-cold water
We are home
I am home
Safe against the dangers
Of the other place

THE LIONESS CIRCLES HER BROOD IN NEW ORLEANS
TO SWIM HOME
(for Marvalene Hughes)

When the storm was coming, the first storm . . . Rita, Marvalene called . . . unhappy. "I have to evacuate the school . . . and I just got here." I made nice noises because Marvalene is a friend . . . an old . . . not aged . . . friend and I could tell she was upset. I am a big fan of when you can't change it, you've got to go with it. "Want me to come down?" I asked trying to offer support. She didn't say "Dummy! If folk could come down I wouldn't be evacuating the school." She just said "No. I'm going to visit my sister. I'll be all right." I watched Rita make land. I tracked her. New Orleans and Dillard had made it through. I remembered Hugo here in Blacksburg when my fifty-pound umbrella weight was sliding across my deck. I was in Florida even before that when Hurricane David penetrated the walls of my condo. So while I was aware of the fear I was still trying to remember we had all gotten through. Then along came Katrina.

Katrina was shaping up to be one of those hurricanes that we all remember. I'm a big Al Gore fan and I was absolutely in awe when I saw his film. This was going to be quite a moment.

My son and I, when he was a little boy, used to visit an island called Young Island which is off the coast of St. Vincent. For the hip folk, Young Island is about a two-hour sail from Mustique which is where Princess Margaret and her friends used to hang out at or near the Cotton House. I never made it to the Cotton House but one night our manager said "There's a tropical depression coming our way. You may want to go on up to your suite after dinner." There were a lot of things to love about Young Island: no phones; no shoes; no roads. Of course, this was before everybody and their mother had a cell phone. You could go there to totally relax. The most dangerous thing in or near the island was a piranha who had been fed so much garbage she was friendly. No worry there. I tried to understand why I would need to go to my room after dinner. The island is quite small. No one is ever around. And why on earth would I worry about the tropical being sad? Isn't that what a depression means? Then it hit.

Lightning thunder winds like I have never seen. Thomas came from his room to "sit with me" but we both were scared to death. Since the island is essentially a rock that has been hollowed out we were safe except for the front window which we got way away from. The next morning when I saw the manager I said something like "Boy! Was that ever a storm!" "Yes," he answered in that way the Brits do when they are coping with a real problem. "It's one of our worst tropical depressions in years. We're all right but St. Vincent was really hard-hit." Now I understood. It was not mental. Katrina wasn't either.

When my phone rang and I heard Marvalene's voice I knew she was upset. "I have to evacuate the campus again!" Yeah, but this time it was going to be real real bad.

The story of Dillard University is a story of courageous leadership. Dillard took the hardest hit of the colleges but Dillard had the strongest person to handle it. *After the Storm* is an important voice to add to the lore of the wrath of Katrina. We need to understand how Marvalene Hughes put her heart on her shoulder and made everyone care that this school survive. It's a great story. And not only because Marvalene is my friend but because she demonstrated the very best of all of us. I had to share with her that the Katrina era was the only time I had wished I was rich. I would have written a check for a million dollars and never looked back. But since I'm a poet I do have books. I culled my personal library for first editions and once the library building was rehabilitated I sent about eleven hundred first editions to help jump-start Dillard's library. I wish I could have done more. But I, and others, gave the measure of what we had. Following Marvalene's lead.

My grandmother's grits
Are so much better than mine

Mine tend to be lumpy
And a bit disorientated
Though that is probably
My fault

I always want
To put 1 cup grits
Into 4 cups cold
Water with 1 teaspoon
Salt
And start them all together

Grandmother did it
The Right Way

She started with cold water
That she brought
To a boil

Shifted the grits slowly
Into the bubbles
Then added her salt

She also hummed
While she stirred
With her wooden spoon

I wonder if I
Should learn
To sing

SPRING BLOOMS

Everyone knows
In Spring love grows
Among the birds and the bees
And the humans too

That squiggly worm
Which makes the soil turn
Also falls in love

The Robin gets up
As an early bird should
To catch a careless bug
But maybe the Robin
Has made a mistake
And simply wanted a hug

At any rate
I need a date
With you to watch the moon bloom
We'll sit and we'll chat
About this and that
And maybe like that owl and that cat
We'll dance by the light of the moon the moon
We can dance by the light of the moon

THE INTERNATIONAL OPEN

(Tennis Players vs. Poets)

tennis players
and poets
talk to themselves
one complaining
of unforced errors
the other lamenting
lovers
not here

poets find wonderful
witty repartee
to captivate
the imagination
of the beloved
tennis players curse
in languages we don't
understand
explaining the loss
of points

poets understand loss
old age marriage
fatigue and well
just not going to
make any sense
to this person
   this time
game point
set point
match point
   no love

The Poet was having a typical day: too much to do with too little time to do it in, yet . . . she was excited. Today she would have a Christmas/Birthday dinner with friends. True, she would have to share the occasion but, hell, if poetry isn't about sharing, what is?

She was up early because she knew she would need a nap in order to stay alert. The Poet is a great napper and heartily recommends it.

She was off first thing to The Giggle Bank. She hadn't been to the Bank since before the Sadness. And because this was a special day she didn't want any thoughts other than happy ones. To be on the safe side she decided to make a substantial withdrawal.

The Giggle Bank requires an appointment. As the Poet sped through town she was willing to risk a ticket because she just couldn't be late. It can be difficult to get an appointment with The Giggle Fairy, since so many people always want to see her. The Poet had had to pull a few strings to be seen on such short notice. She remembered The Giggle Fairy from younger days but they had not seen each other in a while.

Your Mother left you a bunch of Giggles, the Poet was told. Probably a years or so's worth. You never did come back to ask us after she went on her journey to the sky.

I was sad, said the Poet.

The Giggle Fairy was having none of that: Well, we noted you went to the Wyne Bank and made many withdrawals.

Yes, the Poet confessed, and many silly phone calls in the middle of the night seeking a comforting voice.

Had you come to us, GF sternly stated, we could have saved you some embarrassment.

Yes, the Poet acknowledged, and I am working very hard to set things right. That's why this evening is so important to me. May I ask if the Administrator has been in for a withdrawal?

You know we cannot answer that. Nor can we answer if her Wonderful Husband has or has not been in. We are a secure bank, you know.

The Poet appreciated the tip. Then maybe I should get enough for the car and for the dinner.

Where are you going to dinner?

About an hour and a half south. Maybe two hours for dinner. An hour and a half back. I think five hours of Giggles should do us proud.

Well, here you are. And don't forget: You Must Not Leave Any Giggles Just Laying Around.

Are you still having that sale? For every Giggle I use I get two back in the bank?

Yes, of course. Even though you haven't been in that is still the arrangement we made with your Grandmother. What a laffer she was! There were times we would have been out of Giggles but your Grandmother always found a reason to raise a smile. We were hoping you might . . . but never mind. I'm glad you came to us. Enjoy your evening.

The Poet hurried home to quickly nap, shower, dress, and eat a bit. She wanted champagne for the drive and knew she must eat to keep everything on an even keel.

And what a lovely night. The drive down was just about the expected time until the driver got lost. But not for long. The meal was exquisite. The wine wonderful. The service and the company beyond compare. Dinner was not over at nine but rather eleven. And there were still two hours, more or less, to home. Then the unexpected happened.

Everyone had been laughing and giggling and having such a good time that no one realized the Giggles had run out. The Poet should have warned the table but she was so busy laughing she forgot. The Poet knew what would happen: The Administrator would crash on the way home. The Wonderful Husband who had also laughed but who is very protective of the Administrator would not ever have allowed himself to sleep. The Director of a Special Program never slept when she was out. That only left the Poet and the Administrator. Someone had to close her eyes until more Giggles would be obtained.

The Administrator yawned, blinked, and lay her head in the Wonderful Husband's lap. Riding sideways like that would give her bad dreams so she sat up and drifted away. The Poet was enchanted. The Poet was under the impression she was the only one who could sleep sitting up and here we had the Administrator doing it.

Probably it was the trust the Administrator showed when she closed her eyes. She entrusted her Wonderful Husband to the Director and the Poet knowing they would do everything in their power to make him comfortable. Whereas he was, indeed, the only man in the group, the Poet was the only poet so there was outreach. The Administrator leaned back and drifted deeper into a comfortable and safe place. The Poet took that as the highest compliment, since one will do many things with people but sleeping in their presence is a sign of true friendship. The Couple were taken home first. The Administrator awoke and her Wonderful Husband safely escorted her into the house. They blinked the lights to say Good Night.

The Poet and the Director were then dropped off. As the Poet was taking her good clothes off to air and hang up, she, as was her habit, checked her pockets and there, to her surprise, were a couple of leftover Giggles. She remembered now that she had scooped some up when she had gone to the Ladies' Room. Oh, Wow! Had they been brought forward the Administrator would have been allowed to stay awake and Giggle on the way home. Of course, the Poet justified, dinner was two hours longer than expected and there had been plenty of Giggles to go around but these would have made the trip home totally participatory. I should have remembered, the Poet admonished herself. I wonder, as had become a way of life between the two of them, how I can make this up.

She thought and thought, then realized there was nothing she could do. It was a perfect evening. And everyone was happy. So the Poet did a wise thing: she put the Giggles under her pillow and danced and Giggled all through that night in her dreams.

KICK STRETCH KICK

I wish I could
Exercise
While I sit
In class listening
To my students
Pontificate

I would stretch
My legs
And point
My toes
Then lift
Each or the other
To the top
Of the table

No one needs
To know

And I need to lose
Five pounds

Gee whillikers I wish
I could stretch
My mind

I was a Mama's girl. I adored her. The only other person who even came close was Grandmother. I would follow Grandmother so closely that when she stopped I would run into her. But finally it came. I had an older sister, Gary. She would have been Gary Eugene but she was a girl so they changed it to Gary Ann. I am Yolande, Jr., because I was named after my mother. Gary went to school. I actually found that to my liking. Mommy and I would get up and have breakfast with Gary and Gus, our father. Then off they would go and my world would brighten considerably. Mommy and I would wash or iron or, my favorite, dust. We didn't have a car so we walked to the grocery, stopped by to give a holler to friends. And if the day was going well Mommy might play a hand or two of Canasta with Mrs. Morris and Aunt Jeannie. She wasn't really my aunt but a good friend of Mommy's so we called her by that honorific. But it finally came. I knew Mrs. Hicks because she lived across the street from us. Her kids were younger than we were so we didn't play with them but we all knew each other. I probably even knew Mrs. Hicks taught school but it wasn't something I needed to relate to as I didn't go. But it finally came. Mommy woke me up early because I had to bathe and get dressed. I have to tell you I was skeptical. What could be better than staying at home with Mommy? I poked around with my breakfast while Gus and Gary were telling me how much I would enjoy school. I still don't trust it when people are excited about you doing something. *Oh you'll love it* they say knowing full well this will cut your heart out. But I have always prided myself on my bravery. I don't run from physical, emotional, or intellectual fights. I could handle this, I kept saying to myself. But the tears welled up and by the time we arrived at Oak Avenue School they were spilling over. Then Mommy said *Good-bye*. It was too much. I bawled my heart out. Mrs. Hicks, who was the kindergarten teacher, tried to cheer me up and distract me. I was having none of it. But the first-grade teacher, Mrs. Scott, said *Come on, Nikki. You can visit my class.* The irony is that both kindergarten and first grade were in the same room. But I was always a sucker for that kind of logic. When I would fall or stumble Mommy would say *Come here, Nikki, and I'll pick you up.* It worked every time. I took Mrs. Scott's hand and walked to the other side. Mrs. Scott had a physical condition that caused her head to bobble and I think I thought she needed me. She didn't. But I didn't know that. So I guess it's only fair to say my first mentor was Mrs. Scott. She let me think she needed me. And I stayed in school. And all that I have learned and been able to share I think I owe to Mrs. Scott.

I baked it
In a biscuit
And someone came along
While I wasn't looking
And stole it away

I had planned
To take it
For Show-and-Tell
Naked I would unveil
My prize
The moon would dress me
In moon dust

The stars settling over
My head
And you with your arms
Outstretched
Would awake me
Warm
In the light of day
While the night made its way
Into the kitchen
To become
Morning pancakes

IT'S JUST LOVE

it's just love
it won't sweeten
your coffee
or ice your tea

it won't grill
your steak
or bake your crusty bread

it certainly won't
pour your olive oil
over your shredded parmigiano-reggiano cheeses

it might make
you laugh

it's just love
it won't rub
your feet or your back
it won't tousle
your hair
or paint your
fingernails Red

it might make you
want Red
fingernails
though

it's only love

it has no coupon value
though it also does
not expire

just me
just you
just love

yeah
good for nothing
love

throw it away
when you get
tired of it

I would like to see you
Cooking
I would like for you to cook
For me
I would like to see you decide
Upon a menu
Go to the market
And pick the fruit
The vegetables
The fish
I would like to see you smell the fish Test the
    flesh for freshness and firmness
I would like to watch you
In the bakery
In the bakery by the dinner rolls
Deciding: Rolls or Crusty Bread
I would watch you run back
To get the Goat Butter

I would like to be sitting in a corner
And you
Intent upon your meal
Not noticing me
When you go to the wine store
I would watch you wrestle with red or white
White, of course, because it's fish but red
Is Seductive who ever fell in love
Over a glass of white wine

I—uncharacteristically on time—
Would like you to greet me
In a butcher's apron
I would like to watch you greet me only
In an apron

You would ask me to undress
To undress for you
Before I sit down at the beautiful table
Before you hand me my glass
You would ask me to undress
I would like to watch you watch me
Undressing for you
I would like to watch the movement inside the
    apron
As I undress for you
I would like to watch you walk
No
Stroll to your closet
Where you bring out your old buffalo plaid
    dressing gown
Your pilly much-washed dressing gown that
    smells like you
After you brush your teeth
After you shower After you comb your hair
I would like to embrace your odor
Your odor Your essence as we sit down to eat
I would like for you to cook for me
I would like that
Very much

ONE THING

There is only one
Thing better
Than waking up to Ben Webster
blowing
Monday Morning Blues
In my ear

There is only one
Thing better
Than waking up to coffee
    Perking
Bread
    Rising
Bacon
    Frying

There is only one
Thing better
Than a blue sky
Birds chirping
The garbage being picked up
On time

Yeah
Only one
Thing better

I had driven to Buffalo. As a Midwesterner with southern roots driving a car has always been fun and comforting. I had had a 1960 Volkswagen that I had purchased for about six hundred dollars. I was in grad school at the University of Pennsylvania. I was studying Social Work in the hopes of emulating my mother and one of her best friends and an incredible "aunt" to me, Theresa Elliot. All the Social Workers I knew were cool and I had been awarded a scholarship. Unfortunately I was never meant to work in any real sort of system. After a year it was decided by all, respectfully and, I might add, lovingly, that Social Work school was not for me. Through the good offices of a great Social Worker, Louise Shoemaker, I was accepted into the MFA program at Columbia. I had a car, a scholarship, and New York City. Could there be anything better?

Now I was in Langston Hughes territory. I lived in a wonderful apartment building at 84th and Amsterdam. I had exciting neighbors in film, dance, Broadway, and jazz. I was also a bit of a rebel so I knew the young people who were changing the world. I don't care what anyone says: We were the Great Generation. But I lent my car to a friend who took a job in another city and it was towed. I purchased another. But I gave that to my nephew who had other issues and it was totaled. So I purchased a Peugeot diesel which I gave to my sister when she got her 3rd divorce but that would be a few years off.

It was my thought that the MFA program was there to help me/ let me/encourage me to write a book. I did. By the end of my first year. I was ready to receive my degree and go on. Columbia didn't look at it that way so I, degreeless, just went on. We in the Black Arts movement, which wasn't really a movement but a group of people who had similar objectives, took a page from the Beats who had taken lessons from Langston Hughes. Read your work to the People. I wasn't afraid of a job but my thought was if

I could pay the rent, have some food on the table, gas was twenty-five cents a gallon, and something left over for those things that make life fun like Barbados and clothes, then I would be O.K. After my son was born I understood I need a bit more structure than that but still a job seemed so foreign. Get a lecture bureau, I said to myself. So I began to read poetry and lecture.

I had driven to Buffalo because driving is relaxing. No one can get to you. You can think or daydream or sing old songs to yourself that nobody else knows or cares about. I know it wasn't winter because only an idiot would drive to Buffalo in winter but it wasn't summer either. It seems it was after Christmas so I'm thinking spring. But early spring, since I had a remembrance of a heavy jacket. I hadn't had a coat since college but I remember it was important to stay warm.

I arrived at the University, greeted folk, laughed, talked, signed books, those sorts of things when someone came to me with "An Urgent Message: Call your office." I didn't know what the "urgent message" could be: Thomas, my son, hurt himself; Debbie who was babysitting him hurt herself; Wendy, the dog, ran away or something might have been wrong with one of my parents. I really couldn't see anything else. But I knew for certain if I called and found out, I wouldn't be able to go onstage that evening. So I tucked the note in my pocket and did what I had been invited to do. When I got to the hotel I called. My father had had a stroke and was in the hospital. I called Mommy to tell her I was in Buffalo and I'd be home as soon as I could. Being a great believer in peppermint and coffee I checked out of the hotel, got in the car, bought a cup of joe, and hit the road. I made it to Painesville, Ohio, where I pulled over for a couple of hours, then repeated step one and went on to Cincinnati.

It's funny how you can live in a house and never notice things falling apart. Walking through the back door which is always how we entered the house I noticed the floor was not right; the upstairs bathroom had a damp floor; the walls were not dirty, Mommy was a great housekeeper, but needing attention. There was no question of what needed to happen. They needed help. I don't know. It's funny, though not humorous, to see that your parents have grown old. I called Debbie to ask if she would bring Thomas down.

My thought was a couple of months and all would be set right. But it wasn't just the stroke, there was an intestinal cancer. And there was no health insurance. Next step: sell the apartment in New York. I know people think cancer doesn't hurt and people think your insurance co-pay is reasonable but neither is true. 20 percent of cancer will put you into bankruptcy. My first thought was Mommy should divorce him, then he would be eligible for one of the programs. This is over thirty years ago but Mommy would have none of it so we needed a lawyer to get things straightened out. We had known Gloria Haffer for a very long time. She and Mommy were friends. And her dad, Ben, had hired me when I was in high school to work the cash register at his store. Now Gloria was a lawyer considering starting her own firm. We caught the gold ring.

Nothing makes me as nervous as filling out forms and things. All I had to do now, which is a strength of mine, was get the physicalities right. Mommy had taught third grade before she went into Social Work. One of her students, Bobby Hunter, now did construction. When he heard what was happening he came and retiled the bathroom. Rather than paint the walls I convinced Mommy to put wallpaper on them. We both hated the kitchen floor so we put a wood floor in. Things were shaping up. 1168 Congress was a three-bedroom house. Mommy had her room:

Gus, my father, would have his when he came home from the hospital; and Thomas had the third. That left the entire basement to me. It was good space. Friends and I built cabinets, bookshelves, and stuff for a den. The bathroom was papered and made special with photos. The other big room was where I showered and dressed. I should explain. The bathroom was really une toilette and a basin. I found, as I am a lover of antiques, an old claw-footed tub for $25 in Newport, Kentucky. It cost about the same to have it delivered to the basement, a plumber hooked it up, and I had a *Mogambo*-type shower. The washing machine emptied into it. I put a refrigerator down there and I was set. *Essence* magazine came down to do an article on me and photographed the whole house. We looked good. The bedroom was small with no clock and no phone. There was only one rule: If I am asleep . . . Do Not Awake Me. To this day I can and do wake up when I should. If I do not I am either sick or too tired to go on. In either case: Do Not Wake Me Up.

My father was a nervous man. If nothing else, he would tap his foot or wring his hands. He was always in motion. In the spring and summer his yard and garden got his attention. He'd always be outside planting or pulling or doing something. He had a beautiful yard. But in the winter the basement got the brunt of this attention. He would wax and wax the floor. After fifteen or twenty years the buildup was incredible. I kept looking at the floor and it was making me crazy. I guess to some extent I am kin to Gus, too, though I am neither mean nor impatient. As the house was pulling into being a lovely comfortable place again, my part still needed work. One night in what I recognize to be a Gus move, I took a straight razor and began getting the wax up. At first it was only a tile or two, maybe four or six. Then looking at the entire three rooms I knew I'd have to do more. So every night when everyone else was in bed I worked on removing the wax. It wore me out but the wax was yielding.

I am an admirer of many writers and their poems, plays, essays, and novels. I love nonfiction, too. But being in the business I had enough sense to know writers are not the work they produce. You may love a writer's book but meeting the writer can break your heart. Yet I could not resist wanting to meet Toni Morrison after reading *The Bluest Eye*. Maybe reading it two or three times. I was still in New York and I knew she worked at Random House. One day I got up my nerve. "This is Nikki Giovanni, I write poetry, and I wonder if it is possible to speak to Toni Morrison." I was incredibly nervous but then she came on the phone and I had no idea what I wanted to say. She was kind enough to invite me for a drink after work and I must say I was thrilled that she had actually read my work. At that time I didn't drink so a "drink" to me was Campari or coffee. I walked down to Random House and we went somewhere. It seems there were other people there but I don't remember. Toni is a great storyteller and she was telling the table about meeting Muhammad Ali. It was fun.

Of course when *Sula* was published she was on track to do what she did: become one of the greatest novelists of her generation. Whenever I could I would go to her readings and she always said nice things about me. I am not much with phones, though we talked a few times. Then my father had a stroke and I moved to Cincinnati. And began working to restore my mother's home. Details take a lot out of you. I was up in the morning to make breakfast; some mornings I took Mommy to work. Worked on the house. Worked on my poems. Things. Things one does to keep things running smoothly. By habit, which I still have, dinner was started or laid out, while breakfast dishes were being washed.

One day Mommy had not gone to work. I don't know why she didn't. She wasn't sick or anything and it wasn't snowy or icy. It threw my routine off, though. Since I was spending a great part of my night with a straight razor getting wax up I was tired during the day. I was a napper. I still am. I said to Mommy I think I'll take a nap. Thomas came home about four so it would have to have been early enough that I could get an hour in before school was out. Mommy knew the rule. I had just drifted when I heard the phone ring. I knew if it was for me Mommy would take a message. But I heard her footsteps on the stairs. I am not a particularly angry person but I could feel myself working up a lather. "Baby," she almost whispered, "it's for you." "I'm asleep." "But Baby," she timidly insisted, "it's Toni Morrison. You have to get up."

And I did. And this was Toni's question: "I'm thinking about quitting my job and writing full-time. I've been working since I was fourteen years old. What's it like not to have a job? You're the only person I know who doesn't work." I poured a cup of coffee. "You're Toni Morrison. You don't need a job. You're great. Run an ad: WANTED: SOMEONE TO TAKE CARE OF A GREAT NOVELIST. Everyone will answer."

"Do you really think so?" she asked. "Guaranteed," I replied. "I'm a poet. We know these things."

And they each lived happily ever after.

DAY PASS TO HEAVEN

Gus Giovanni   Yolande Giovanni

(1914–1982)   (1919–2005)

My father who seldom got things what I would call "right" hit the jackpot when courting my mother: He brought her *A Bell for Adano* which she loved. Or maybe she just loved the idea that a man would think to bring a book. Being on a winning track he gave her *A Tree Grows in Brooklyn*. She married him. And my big sister was born. I always say that the reason a couple has another child is that the first one needed if not perfection a bit of tweaking. My sister heartedly disagreed but they had me anyway. I may not have been an improvement but I did love, do love, to read. No matter what else is wrong in the world a book will take you away from it. My sister was a reader too but she never liked to discuss the characters. My mother did. And so do I.

My favorite story that Mommy would read to me was "King of the Golden River." I recognize it now as a parable but I loved it. And would read it to myself when I learned to read. Gluck's brothers were so mean. I loved it that they turned to stone. Mommy's favorites were things like *Gone with the Wind* or *All This and Heaven, Too*. I was reading from her library by the fifth grade.

But it wasn't until the discovery of Toni Morrison that we both found a book we could talk about and truly explore: *Sula*. Mommy found Toni on her own and asked me, excitedly, had I heard of her? I was pleased to say "I know her." Mommy and I read and reread *Sula* through the years.

As Mommy was drifting away from this world I sat on her bed and wrote poetry to ease the pain of losing her and alternately read *Sula* to her aloud until my tears blocked the words. We had come full circle. I'm sure my father, who didn't get things what I would call "right" very often, got a Day Pass to Heaven and was waiting for Mommy with a cold beer and a book for them to share.

MY DREAM

(for Maya)

You said: this is Nikki's dream
And I thought Yes
But My Dream is to make it
Your dream 2

To find the poets
Standing hand in hand
Embracing novel
Ideas

We grow from such
Dreams even
Though we mostly
Dream at night

I like being
The moon
To your sun
In Toni's spiral Milky Way

let me die
in a bowl
of artichoke soup
from Guy Savoy
surrounded by garlic
cloves and zucchini
blossoms
please wash me down
with a 2002 Ramey Cab

I love the bread tray
too
as long as a block
I'll have the lemon
bread and the seaweed rye
tucked under my arms
my smile will be
enhanced
by goat butter
my sautéed quail
is floating in

I know
I know
I have to go one day
so please let it be
in pureed artichoke
no oil
no wine
just pure springwater
artichoked
soup

This poem was a love poem to my grandmother. I spent my summers with my grandfather and grandmother and ultimately lived with them during my high school years. I was born in Old Knoxville General Hospital; the first person in my family not born at home. I am a Tennessean by birth and that proud state has produced, nurtured, and helped create a lot of writers, composers, and even a statesman or two. I am from Appalachia. The Tennessee mountains with the early evenings and that great morning light made storytellers out of all of us. From Davy Crockett and his "bear" tales to James Agee to Dolly Parton. Parton is also a great businesswoman so her contributions reach beyond her art. I think you always write what you love. Whether it's your grandmother or gourmet cooking or mountains and rivers. Sunsets kissing the tallest building or chipmunks scattering off to bed. I like the quiet. And I like the sound of the quiet. I'm a mountain girl. I listen and make lists of what I hear.

AFFIRMING MY BIRTH DATE

Though I Have No Intention of
Running for Any Public Office

I became concerned because I know you spend a lot of time on the Web and you have discovered a lot of things about me that even I didn't know and actually hadn't questioned. For example, a few years ago you uncovered my real birth year so I quite naturally became concerned when you once again asked: *Was I am I sure that I was born on June 7th?* I wanted to ask my mother when you first questioned me but you had given me such a lovely box of stationery that I feared were you to be proven correct you might ask for its return though ultimately I could find no one so worthy of the note cards that I manufactured reasons to send notes to you. Now that they are gone I am trying to be a woman about this and face facts: *I might actually have been born on June 6th.*

Unfortunately, the family has used up our allotment of Day Passes for this quarter so I could not zip up to ask Mommy and as you had pointed out she was probably not watching either the time or the day. I know it was at 6:00 A.M. that I first drew my breath on my own but that was only because I was upset that Dr. Presnell hit me. Even then I found beating the life into infants was cruel and unusual punishment making it a federal case but Mommy stuck something in my mouth preventing me from making my case. It would be twenty-six years before I remembered to bring that up again.

But thank goodness the Fates are kind when Mother Nature and others of her ilk are hard-nosed. The Fates allowed me to call my grandmother who actually turned out to be the woman I needed to ask, since she was not engaged in the distraction of my beginning journey nor the anxiety my mother was probably experiencing while I began it.

Grandmother remembers looking at her watch because she only had two watches in her life and Grandpapa had given her this one on their fortieth anniversary. Grandmother always adored, and that should be in capital letters, two things that were in a nonreciprocal relationship with her: Racehorses and Diamonds. She was madly in love with my grandfather, adored her three daughters, and, I think, took some pleasure in her six grandchildren but the capital letters still go to Racehorses and Diamonds. Her eyes would glaze over in ways I have no words for. Grandpapa couldn't handle horses after they moved to Knoxville from Albany, Georgia. *If Louvenia wanted horses she should not have sassed that white woman,* he would laughingly say to me. I knew to keep out of it. But diamonds were another matter. As nationalistic as she was she could justify diamonds because they come from Africa so she looked at it as a rescue mission. One of the reasons I have never sought a Day Pass to talk with my sister is she took Grandmother's diamond rings that my mother wore all her life and gave them to Thomas. Of course, it goes without saying I can purchase a diamond ring or earrings or things like that but to me it was never the diamond, it was that I know he saved up for them; earning extra money tutoring Latin and being a Poll Watcher and serving on the Grand Jury. Of course, I recently read they are no longer going to pay folk to be on the Grand Jury which I think will mean folk will decline to do so but that is not our question here. I am a big fan of paying citizens to do good things but I natter which I do not intend to do.

I was born on June 7th because Grandmother was there holding Mommy's hand. My father was there uncharacteristically being supportive until he saw he had another girl and then turned to my aunt Agnes and said: *Ag, ain't she ugly?* Not really a question but seeking an affirmation of what his heart, I had to hope, and not his eyes, saw. I heard him. People forget even folk in deep comas hear what is being said. I knew Gus and I would face difficulties but at that point my grandmother, having allowed Dr. Presnell to beat me and Mommy to stuff something in my mouth to keep me from cursing the doctor out, said: *I like her. Name her after you.* And Mommy did. And I proudly carried that name until Mommy moved to Heaven. When I got to officially name myself. I am Nikki. Born June 7, 1943. No matter what the Web or the Birthday Fairies think. I am me.

THE AMERICAN VISION OF ABRAHAM LINCOLN
ON THE LINCOLN MEMORIAL
150 Years After Lincoln
70 Years After Marian Anderson

At this moment

Resting in the comfort of the statue
Of the 16th president of the United States
Missing
An equally impressive representation
Of his friend and adviser
Frederick Douglass

We come

On this day

Recalling the difficult and divisive war
We are compelled
       With a prayer in the name
         Of those captured and enslaved
       Who with heart and mind
         Cleared the wilderness
       Raised crops
         Brought forth families
       Submitted their souls
         Before a merciful and great God
To acknowledge that The Civil War
Was fought not to free the enslaved
  For they knew they were free
But to free the nation
  From a terrible cancer eating at our hearts

At this moment

In which we are embarrassed
By the Governor of our fifth largest state
   Who appoints a man to the United States Senate
   To which both he and his minion agree:
      The Letter of the Law
      Is more important than
      The Spirit of the Law

Now

When we are dismayed that the accidental
Governor of the Empire State can find
Just one more reason to rain pain
And rejection on a family that has offered only
Grace and graciousness

After two hundred years
When we rejoice that another son
Of the Midwest has offered himself
His wife and his two precious daughters
To show us a better way

We gather

In recognition and understanding
That today is always and forever today
Allowing us to offer this plea
      For light
      And truth
      And Goodness

Forgiving as we are forgiven
Being neither tempted nor intolerant of those who are

We come

At this moment
To renew and refurbish
The American vision
Of Abraham Lincoln

12 February 2009

I am at that point
In life
When I reread
Old books
Bake my mother's favorite recipes
Snuggle with a sneezy quilt
Listen to my old rock and roll records
Feel comfortable
And comforted in my old nearly ragged bathrobe
I am keeping my house shoes
With the hole in the bottom
Though I no longer wear them
And yes the smell is long gone
From that bottle of Joy
Which still sits on my bathroom dresser
Embracing the old things
Is a good new thing
Like kissing you again
And not really paying attention
To whether or not
The Redskins score

I HATE MONDAYS

I hate Mondays
And Tuesdays
And especially Wednesdays
And Thursdays
I despise Fridays
   because Friday nights come
And Saturdays
   in the evening
When other folk are getting
   Bathed
And smelling good
And dressing in something red
And smiling
I have a special place
   in my heart to hate
I'm not fond of Sundays either
And every day of the week
Is awful
I hate whole months too
And seasons
Do I ever hate Seasons
Spring when everything is new
Summer with its salty sweat
Autumn when the gathering starts
And that winter cuddle
I hate it
I hate hours too
And minutes
I even hate seconds
I hate it all
'Cause I really hate
Not being in love
With you
Anymore

A SONG FOR A BLACKBIRD
(for Carolyn Rogers 10-4-10)

We look for words:
    intelligent intense
    chocolate warm
    ambitious cautious

to describe a person

We design monuments:
    the Pyramids   the Taj Mahal
    the Lincoln Memorial   the Empire State
      Building
    the Wrigley Building   Coffins

to say someone was loved

We sing a sad blue
    Song
We sing a river—no—bridge
    Song
We sing a Song of a Blackbird
    To say

You will be missed

I lived on Burns Avenue in Wyoming. I attended Oak Avenue School. I usually walked from Burns to Pendery to Oak Avenue. It was a beautiful school. We had swings and monkey bars and a baseball and kickball field. And I think my favorite memory is Mrs. Scott, who was my first- and second-grade teacher, taking us into the school ground one morning showing us how to pick dandelion greens. We took them back in, cleaned them, and put them on to boil. We had sour milk that we churned into butter while others were making corn bread. That was lunch one day and it was wonderful.

School in those days had morning break where you had a half pint of milk and shortbread cookies, recess where you could play, and though we had "graduated" from nap time we still got afternoon break, then home. Home was, for me, a few chores and home-work. Actually, I finally landed a job because Aunt Lil would let me wash her dishes for, I think, a quarter a week. I thought I was needed but ultimately got old enough to understand she was just trying to be a good aunt.

One winter it seemed it just snowed and snowed. I was a little girl so I don't actually remember the ins and outs but Oak Avenue School ran out of coal. We would have to go to Wyoming High over on Wyoming Avenue.

There was a walk that was a shortcut but it was not a place we went to very often. Usually, if we were going to that section of Wyoming we walked all the way down Burns and turned left. I walked to school with my sister most days and there were other friends along the way. We didn't realize why our parents seemed so upset. We would all just sort of meet up and go to Wyoming High for a couple of days. I think we didn't have a real sense of segregation at that time; we just looked at it as something new. But everyone kept telling us so often how to behave and what we might run into and to do well in classes that they probably made us nervous. We bundled up and went. I don't have a memory of those class days other than playground. We, the Oak Avenues, all stood together wondering what we should do when a couple of kids came over and asked us to play ball.

Time would bring different attitudes but at that point Wyoming High welcomed Oak Avenue and we played together. I like to think friendships were made. If *Icarus* had existed then we would have written poems. And celebrated our differences.

WHEN THE GIRL BECAME A POET

(after Garret Keizer)

when the girl became
a poet
she was so happy

now she could sing her own song
tell the tales of her people

be a truth giver
contribute
something beautiful and useful to the world

unfortunately

the New Order declared the Arts
an enemy
so she went underground
and became a stealth professor

when the student became
a poet
he was delighted

he took to smoking a pipe
and wearing frayed jackets

more and more he was

unfortunately

incomprehensible
and if there was light in his truth
the smoke coming off that place
obscured it

but he was so full of himself he ceased
eating
and was last seen lying
in a gutter
reading a ten-year-old
review of his chapbook

when the clouds became poets
they formed beautiful sentences
in the blue and sometimes at night
using the contrails

there was mystery and amazement
and people were up all night long
deciphering the message
of the clouds

unfortunately

the bat . . . too . . . had become
a poet
and she had a tale to tell of flying
by the scent of fresh fruit
sort of like Columbus sailing
on his Search for Spices

the bat dodged Owls
and the nets of scientists
while sharing her verses aloud

unfortunately

she cried
when she realized poems
were her true calling

not night flights nor
evading predators

but she was such a fragile creature
with no pockets like the kangaroo
nor folds like the walrus

she was vulnerable
to the vestiges of
wind and weather

she feared for the pride
she took in her muse

her fear turned
to depression
and she drank herself
to an early death
by carelessness around
a ten-year-old boy with a slingshot

When God made mountains
He made runaway slaves
With no book knowledge of the North Star
Nor botany classes describing moss
On the north side of trees

He made black men and women unafraid
Of mountain lions and Florida
Panthers and no matter what
Teddy Roosevelt tried to show: bears
do not like people
   not the cuddly little Koala
   not the fierce Grizzly
   not the mighty Polar
   nor the humble mountain
Black bear . . . all bears and their dens
Are to be avoided

God did make the jackrabbit who could be snared
God made the possum who is slow
God made the clever raccoon
And rivers sweet with fish

He made berries and nuts and green leafy things
Which were safe and good
To eat

When God made runaway slaves
He knew they would need a friend
Not only in nature
But of a human kind
So he sent Mountaineers
He sent white people who would not be a slave
Nor own one

Who would not kill a slaveholder
Nor die for one
He sent a free white man
Who believed in change
And a free white woman who believed in him
And they made their home
Amid these mighty mountains

They liked to have a drink or two
So they welcomed Johnny Appleseed
Who brought stories and fermented applejack
They liked heroes so they welcomed the traveling
    preacher
With his message of a man "who has trampled
    out the vineyard
Where the grapes of wrath are stored"
They liked to sing so they welcomed
The runaway slave with his banjo
And friendships were formed

When God made mountains he made men and
    women
Who would need each other
Who would respect each other
Who would carry the Word so that all men
And women could be saved

When God made mountains
He said "Come unto me, ye who need rest"
And they called it Appalachia, the Original Word
For Peace
And some folk said: This cannot be Done
And the rest said: Yes we Can
And the clouds settle in that welcome place

Between ground and trees and sky
   Like smoke coming off a coffeepot
   Like steam coming from a kettle of pinto beans
   Like the rustic smell of a wood-burning fire at
      day's end
At home and at peace
Like God has a rocking chair in the sky
Smoking his pipe
And being proud
Of His Great Smoky Mountains

THESE WOMEN

I have known these women
Have loved and admired them
Have been afraid of and for them

I have slept on lumpy double beds
That were covered with quilts
Made by these women and their friends
Washed in a communal tub
And dried with kisses from the Tennessee breeze
The dreams I have dreamed under those quilts
Took me on this journey not yet completed

I have sat with these women
On back porch steps
Gutting Catfish or Whiting
My knife flying up and down
Split exactly to the center the better to lay flat
In the hot grease of the skillet

My hair covered in fish scales
My hands covered with blood
My lips smiling as I have been welcomed
Into the company of women

My grandmother would let me
Break the green beans
Pop pop pull the string though
When guests were expected she
Would "French" them
That was a kitchen job

Saturday was a cleaning day
I have bent to my knees to scrub
The wooden pantry floor

And climbed on shaky chairs
To Pledge the cabinets in which are kept the
　good dishes

Sundays were Sunday School and Church
Our Sunday best clothes
Our deliverance from and to
Sunday was the answer
I did not know then
The question

I have heard these women
When they thought I was asleep
Crying for their sons
In jail
Or their daughters
Being beaten
I have seen the bruises of the daughters
And I have seen the grandmothers
Not looking

I have heard their prayers when they didn't know
What to pray for
Looking for understanding and relief
Praying for their granddaughters to not
Make the same mistakes

Had there been magic
I would have lifted these women
All of them
Into a red cape
And sprinted them away to a happy land

But they are grounded
In their God and their families
They are grounded in their hearts and minds

They majestically knew

They are grounded in me

And here I stand
With arms wide open
A song fleeing
from my breasts
from the goodness
Of our grandmothers

And I must sing

After my father had a stroke my son, our dog, and I moved back home from New York to Cincinnati to help my mother. Always being a mama's girl it was a natural thing to do. Plus I must admit I hate it when people know you need help and then make you ask. There was no way taking care of a stroke victim would be easy so we moved. First I put a fence in the backyard for the dog, then turned the garage into a tree house without a tree for my son and the friends I knew he would make. That turned my attention to the house.

It was a nice house. FHA-type house. Small but enough room. We needed a porch, since decks and porches are so different. We had one put on which extended the living room and cooled the house better. My father was an Alabaman by birth and he loved sitting on the porch and calling out to his neighbors. Lincoln Heights is a country town where folks do that sort of thing. Everyone was doing O.K.

Mommy still was working which I hoped she would continue to do until he was on his feet. Mommy tended to feel sorry for her husband, my father, and she would cut his meat, make his bed . . . things like that. I thought he should do for himself. If I could keep her working he would. That would be another story for another time.

I don't eat breakfast. There is probably some deep meaning or perhaps trauma about that but I don't eat breakfast. I am not necessarily disdainful of breakfast but it seems awfully early to put food on the table let alone in your mouth. My first meal of the day to start is dinner. Dinner is my favorite. You can sit down recognizing there is nothing important that you need to do. You can relax. While I was helping Mommy that was what I did: the same as if I were in my own home. I start dinner. It actually got to the point that when my father awoke if there was nothing on or in the stove he would ask where we were going that evening because he understood the pattern.

One of my favorite restaurants then was a little Bistro called Le Central. It is French. In downtown San Francisco. Le Central kept a pot going and they would post on the board how many days the pot was still stirring. They sometimes got several months. The pot works this way: You keep your vegetables in the pot and add water or wine or, I suppose, beer. No meat. Mommy and I got to laughing one day and we decided we would start a frontier pot. Mommy and I had been having a very very low-grade argument about saving grease. I said No. She said Yes. I would throw the grease out; she would hide it in the back of the fridge. We finally called a truce: the frontier pot. Mommy thought I was wasteful because I throw things out; I thought she was foolish to keep teeny tiny leftovers. This was a good compromise.

I think it started with peas. No. First you need a clean gallon jar with a top. Then the leftover veggies of the day. Peas. Corn. Squash. Whatever you have left over. Ziplock bags are important because you might want to save the juice. If you, for example, boil potatoes, the water has nutrients in it but you don't want to save the water with the veggies or they will get soggy. I saved 2 cups liquid in ziplock bags which I froze. Then when I needed to add liquid I could, in 2-cup amounts. Anything can go in the frontier pot. Pasta. Tomatoes. Anything you have. We kept it going for 30 days, then we made soup. To be honest it drove my father and son crazy. They hated Saturdays when Mommy and I would say Oh Frontier Pot for dinner. Of course we made a nice green salad and warm bread, usually corn bread, and we tried to make it very nice with bread pudding for dessert because even though we were four people it still is very hard to eat a loaf of bread. What I did was freeze the leftover bread so that we could have fresh bakery bread most of the time. My son learned to hate frozen bread, too, but we can't always get to the bakery. Bread pudding is the easiest thing on earth so the house smelled good. And let's be honest: If this is all you're getting, then you may as well enjoy it. Sometimes when we finished off the Pot and had to start again, we wrote the number of days on the refrigerator; sometimes we had a little left over and the day count would continue. It was fun. I still put stock in the freezer and when I make soups or beans I pull out my ziplock and think of the good times I had cooking with my mother.

P.S.: I recognize this has no recipe but it is a living thing. It's fun to try, especially in winter. It does keep you from wasting "a little bit." And with herbs, spices, and a bit of beer or wine it's wonderful.

WHAT THE FLY ON THE WALL OVERHEARD AND TOLD A FRIENDLY YELLOW FINCH WHO MENTIONED IT TO A LONELY BAT AS SHE SET OUT ON A CLEAR, DRY EVENING TO SEARCH FOR RIPE FRUIT

Or

Happy Birthday, Nancy

The Department Head was hurrying to close her door against the ravages of demands when she heard a whimper. Or perhaps it was a sigh. But whatever it was it was undeniable: Someone needed help. She turned toward the sound. "I am having a birthday soon," said the Associate Head, "and it makes me feel so old." "Oh," said the Department Head, "you shouldn't feel old. There are lots of people here older than you." "No," insisted Nancy. "No one is older than I. Some people have been here longer but I am the oldest person in the world!" "Oh, no," declared the Department Head. "Look at Nikki. No one is older than Nikki."

"Are you sure?" Nancy said. "Nikki always looks so chipper and vibrant."

"Yes, I know," said the Department Head, "but I looked it up. Nikki is way older than she knows. There was a mix-up in her birth records. She thinks she was born in 1943 but she was actually born in 1439. No one knows how to explain this to her so she still gets a birthday every year.

"I know this," the Department Head continued, "because two years ago I forgot her birthday and received a blistering message from *The Birthday Fairies*. They made it very clear that if I ever did that again they would take away not only *my* February date but my husband's December. That Birthday calendar is very strict."

"Well," Nancy asked, "do you think Nikki is planning to live forever?"

"I have to say," said the Department Head, dimples resting in their arches, "it really looks like it. If she accepted her age now the entire Civil War not to mention the War of the Roses and . . . Good Gracious! Think of the love affairs . . . financial things . . . discoveries that would have to be undone. No, I think the best thing is to let it be."

"But aren't there people in Heaven waiting for her?" asked Nancy.

"Well. I'm not so sure of the location," said the Department Head, "but Bandit has been in touch with Wendy who is enjoying Nikki's mother's company. They were just joined by Nikki's former babysitter so the beer and the talk is flowing. Wendy misses Nikki. Don't tell her that, though. It would make Nikki sad."

"So what should we do," Nancy asked, "about June 7th?"

"I think I'll make her a quiche. She really likes my quiches."

"But should someone that old eat that many eggs? It might kill her."

"Well," said the Department Head, "we all have our jobs, don't we?" She turned to present a box to Nancy. "And here is my very best Red Velvet Cake for you!"

"So it's O.K. for me to go ahead with my birthday?"

"Yes, Nancy. Happy Birthday. And many many more."

The End

I think fear should be a spice. Something we sprinkle on our steaks just before we put them on the grill; something we mix in with our corn muffins and bake at 350 degrees for twenty minutes or until golden brown. Maybe we take fear leaves to decorate our apple pie right out of the oven . . . not before or the leaves will burn and not look nearly so pretty. I'm thinking if we can learn to distill fear we have two wonderful preparations: perfume for smells and alcohol for ingestion.

Perfume carries its own scent of danger and excitement but when we throw a little *Fear* in there things really heat up. Ask John Edwards or Herman Cain and see if I'm not right. *Fear: The Scent He Can't Resist.* We'd have to find an exclusive outlet for it. We wouldn't want everybody to be able to get their hands on it. I'll have to form a committee to find that solution. Maybe the White House has some ideas. Or . . . oh yes . . . The Tiger Woods Emporium! *Get Your Fear Right Here.* You can practice your swing, whatever that might mean, while your bottle is bagged.

And if we made it drinkable we'd probably have a light green liquid with its own two-ounce top. You can take your fear on the rocks . . . or slip a bit of coke in there to make it mighty smooth. We could get the Culinary Channel to feature Fear at one of the drink offs and we'd reward the best new barista with his and her very own gold bottle of Fear to be used anytime they'd like.

I need to explain right here, it's not fear that causes problems, it's when hatred is combined with it. Fear on its own tells you not to lend your cousin money; don't go down that dark street, girl; take yourself home from this party now. Fear is a warning signal. Healthy. Good idea. That fish smells funny. My dog does not like this man. Fear is a good thing. It's why I want to keep it exclusive. If everyone can have fear then we have to cut it. Like drugs. It's not the cocaine that kills you it's the stuff they cut it with to make the drugs go further. You don't want pure fear but you don't want it cut with hatred either. Hatred is a bad idea. Which is why it's cheap and available anywhere you look.

Maybe what will really work is we all need to have a fear tree in our backyard or a small fear plant growing on our apartment windowsill. When we are feeling uneasy we pluck a few leaves and find the right place to put them. Champagne would be the number one choice but spaghetti works, too. Have a little Fear at least once a week and you will build up your resistance. Like a vaccination. Then when wars and hatreds come along you'll be able to recognize that's just another expression of Fear. No thanks, I've had my quota.

That's what I'm thinking we really need: An Antidote for Fear.

BISCUITS: DROPPED OR BAKED

First you harvest the laughter
Local is best
But sometimes you need nationwide
To really get the bellows

Mix a bit of dirt
Not the serious hurting kind
But the kind you'll find in the beauty
Parlor or barbershop
Parlor parlay biscuits
All the same

Then gently fold in some grandmother love
There is always a bit of grandmotherly
Love somewhere
Some days though I will admit
It can be more difficult to find
Than others

Call a girlfriend for "Dropped"
Or an old love for "Baked"
Either way you'll know when they're done

Oops! We forgot the salt
You can laugh till you cry
Or cry till you laugh
The salt will come

Crispy Brown Ready

Serve them warm
Remembering summer mornings before Church
Or Saturday evenings with fried fish

Biscuits always bring memories
Of home

POETS

Poets shouldn't commit
Suicide
That would leave the world
To those without imaginations
Or hearts

That would bequeath
To the world
A mangled syntax
And no love
Of champagne

Poets must live
In misery and ecstasy
To sing a song
With the katydids

Poets should be ashamed
To die
Before they kiss
The sun

FOR MARK DRESSMAN

Who would have thought
There would be / could be a button
On the wall
Where when you touch
The room lights up
Electricity didn't build
On the candle
It replaced wax

Who would want to believe
Human beings could sit
On a Hydrogen Bomb
(we call it a Space Ship)
   and sail off into Space
   and walk on the moon
   and land a surrogate on Mars
Just to Marvel! at the unknown
And why wouldn't
We want to take what is
   Known
And add what is
   Wonderful
And let the poems flow
   From tears of laughter
   From sweat of work
   From the deliciousness of tomorrow
To the knowledge of Today

Grant me that A implies B
B necessitates C
C calls for D
And eventually
You and I will get an Alphabet

Grant me that Curiosity implies Research
Research requires Reading
Reading delights the heart
And you and I will get a voice

Grant me Love implies
   not desire but
Commitment
Commitment accepts Challenge
Challenge embraces Theory
And you and I will get Reason: A way to explore
                                        past actions
                                          and
                                        future dreams

Good for us
On your Mark Dressman
Get Ready!
Let's Poem!

A little calf
Dancing in the rain
Unaware of the joy
She brings me

I speed along at 70 mph
Trying to get home

The baby colt asleep
In the sweet grass
Mother patiently watching
Over him

I am packing my bags
For London

Trafalgar Square
Silver-faced mime
A war throwing kisses
Couples laughing
I wish I wish I wish
You were here

Dear Editor:

I write in defense of flowers. It seems that lately everyone wants to put flowers in competition with other good works. Someone will die and the family will say "in lieu of flowers," which seems unfair to me. It should be "in addition to flowers . . ." Flowers and the florists who make them into beautiful sculptures are not some adjunct to our occasions. We wouldn't dream of marrying without flowers no matter how small a bouquet nor how elaborate a setting. What would February 14th be without flowers for the ones you love? And Mother's Day! Could there beat a heart so cold that there is for Mother a . . . what . . . electric skillet, "in lieu of flowers"? But florists cannot just count on one or two days a year for a business. Florists purchase flowers that a flower farmer has nourished from seed, then harvested, then transported to shops where they then fill your loving request. Florists hire people to work with and for them, keeping a small business going in these difficult times. What are we saying when we say insurance companies and predator lenders are too big to fail—that florists and other boutique businesses are too small to succeed? Why is it the minute we want to save money we cut out the arts and flowers? I know that some will say "Well, what do we do with the flowers when the event is over?" We use these wonderful gifts of nature to comfort us when we bury the departed; we use them to celebrate our special occasions; we use them to say "I love you" to a beloved. They then can travel from our hearts to hospitals comforting the ill and injured; they can visit with the Ladies of the Red Hats to add joy to their meetings; they can be shared with an elderly neighbor on a fixed income who would welcome the extravagance. Some will surely say "But we need charitable contributions." Indeed we do. I cheer for charity all the time. But there is a need for flowers as surely as there is a need for hummingbirds. Some things are wonderful on their own; enchantment is reason enough. I remember when my mother passed five years ago a friend who had been in Thailand learned late of her passing and sent a beautiful bird-of-paradise almost a year after the event. I confess: A note saying *A Tree Has Been Planted Somewhere* would not have been as comforting. And I could dry it and press it into the memory book as "The Last Flower." Not "in lieu of flowers." No. In addition. Because flowers neither reap nor sow they are perfect for mourning and rejoicing. Flowers sing a silent song that says: "I really care." Flowers are the "Honey, I'm home" when work is put aside; "Good Night, Sweetheart" at the end of the day; the sigh at the end of a kiss. Why should we deny ourselves the beam of the moon against the quiet sky? Why should we privilege anything over the fragrance of love?

WEREWOLF AVOIDANCE

I've never "blogged" before
so this is new
territory for me I do
poet though and that
is always somewhere in
the *netherland* I think
poetry is employed
by truth I think
our job is to tell
the truth as we see it don't you
just hate a namby-pamby poem that goes
all over the place saying nothing

Poets should be strong
in our emotions
and our words that might make us
difficult to live with but I do believe
easier to love
Poet is garlic
Not for everyone
but those who take it
never get caught
by werewolves

EXERCISE

I want to ride
On a train

I sometimes fly
In a jet plane

I love to cruise
In a big boat

I'd even float
In a green moat

Of course I could always
Bike

And for health reasons
Hike

But if I had my druthers

I'd get my exercise

In your arms

I COMMUNICATE

I communicate
With you
In the dark
I am a shadow
At eventide
A white piece of chalk
On a white blackboard
I am a blackberry
On a bear's purple tongue
I am a pebble in your oil tank
Flush me out
You will run smoother
But with not nearly as much fun
Bumping
Moves us all along

I fly away at morning
To await your sleep
I will sneak in
Too dark
Too quiet
Too loving
For you to say
No More
I don't want a shadow
I want you

I watched *The Visitor*

They
Like boys shaking salt on slugs
Chased
Deported
Misunderstood
The pain
Were indifferent to
The lives
They were destroying

They tried to convince
Me
They were protecting
Me
Those boys
Who explained
Why they were throwing
Stones at mother robin
Breaking her wing
And preventing not her flight
But her ability to feed
Her three little hatchlings
Who are condemned to death
By starvation
They laughed
In nazi-ese
They were only doing
Their jobs

What pitiful
Little gerbils
We have
Become

We live
To keep others
From living

I saw *The Visitor*
Play his drum
While Sarah Palin
Field-dressed a moose
And encouraged her daughter
To have sex
With her oldest son
Sarah was
After all
Too busy at the PTA
Explaining what *abstinence* means

Oh boy
What ecstasy

I am embraced
With lies
And hypocrisy

Hug me, Baby
Do it Good

I am an American
My life
Is a fucking prison

Hi Ho, Silver
Away!!!!

Here we stand
Negotiating
That space
Between I'm in love
With you
And let's be friends

This will not turn out well

I need a guitar
Or a good drunk
Or something ugly
To find
The song
In these blues

Let's get a twelve-string
Banjo
And sing a song
For runaway slaves

MY DIET

If you are what you eat
I'm definitely having an exciting poem
For breakfast

Lunch will be a mean metaphor
With lots of rhythm on the side
Pounding that baked beat
To say what's on my mind

Dinner is a more sedate affair
A simile with a little sweetness
For dessert
And that should make for something
Exciting to come
Out of me
In the morning

Saturdays were tedious because there were always chores which didn't actually take that long but after lunch (which I always enjoyed with Grandmother) I had to go to the beauty parlor. As a kid I didn't mind but when I got to be 14 or 15 I had other things to prepare for. Of course, many of my friends who were boys would go swimming on summer afternoons and most of us who were girls would sit and watch. Even with swimming caps our hair would get wet and "go back" so we stood or sat on the sidelines. The crazy thing about all that was if there was a dance at The Phillis Wheatley Y you also couldn't "slow drag" because the boys would be sweaty against your face and your hair would get wet and "go back." It goes without saying that we were not allowed to slow drag.

But having survived all that, we awakened to wonderful Sunday mornings. We attended Mt. Zion Baptist Church where grand-papa was a Deacon and Grandmother helped with Sunday School and other things. I remember she wasn't an Usher and she didn't sing in the choir, though she had a beautiful voice, nor did she play the piano or organ, though she could do both.

I wasn't actually paid for chores, since I slept and ate there, but Grandpapa would give me a quarter or sometimes a bit more for Sunday School and church. I'm a big fan of "rendering" so I didn't actually mind putting money in both times but finally my grand-mother realized I had nothing left to go for ice cream with the other kids and she kind of directed me to "share" with God but not give it all. Ice cream is important, too. Peach, for her. Vanilla, for me.

Bonnie, Joanne, David, and the rest would leave Sunday School at about 10:30 A.M. and walk down to Carter-Roberts Drug Store. Church didn't start until 11:00. Carter-Roberts had a juke-box where a quarter would get you six songs which individually would be a nickel apiece. We all chipped in. It was Nina Simone. *Live at Central Park* I think. She was singing "I Loves You, Porgy."

I already was and remain a big fan of *Porgy and Bess*. I can under-stand, though I disagree with, the folk who disliked *Amos 'n' Andy*. I could see it was important to see Black folk on TV and, to be fair, it was funny. Maybe not funny in the rerun called *Good Times* and certainly not funny in the sequel called *The Jeffersons* but *Amos 'n' Andy* worked for me at that time. *Porgy and Bess* even I, a kid, knew was important. It is classic. And if you loved, as did I, mythology, *Porgy and Bess* fit right in. Let me confess: I never actually believed George Gershwin wrote all that music.

I believed Gershwin spent a lot of time "uptown" to learn to translate the music that became *Rhapsody in Blue*. I grant him total control of *An American in Paris*. But *P and B*? No way. "Summer-time" could be heard anywhere the Black community was giv-ing thanks for another season. The rhythms are all gospel. Even the chants. "Strawberry Woman." No way. And Nina Simone reclaimed it for us. She brought that southernersness but on a sophisticated level to us. We all loved her.

Our last nickels, having forgone ice cream, went to Nina. And we were satisfied.

So you can imagine the thrill I felt when I walked into Mich-aux's bookstore in Harlem one fall afternoon and Nina Simone was there! I didn't even try to be cool about it. I love you!!! I gushed. She was very nice about it. That Nina Simone had read my book was beyond compare. I was over the top. My mother was coming to town and I was having a party to show Mommy that I have friends and I'm all right. I invited Nina. My thought was this: Prob-ably most people are fans so they think the star is always busy doing glamorous things so the star never gets invited to do things with ordinary folk. I gave her my address and phone number. And left.

She came. My mother was thrilled. So was everybody else. Nina was good people. I'm proud to call her my friend.

We sit like Sally Walker
In a circle trying
To spin something wonderful
On this loom hoping
Maybe a magic dwarf
Will come to show
Us where the gold is

We sit in here together
Not in a square nor
Rectangle
But the triangle between right wrong and really
Who cares

Facebook says I have friends
Friends say strange things
Avoiding my face

There is a star
Which is not me
Though it should be
On a hill
It shines on Henry Street
Where Duke Ellington played
Where Nat "King" Cole sang
Where dancers danced
The blues away:
The segregation blues
The you can't go here or come there blues
The evil blues played on a stolen banjo
The railroad blues that strummed the lines
While the Pullman Porters called **George** by some
Called **Honey** by some
Called **Daddy** by some

Called **Grandpop** swayed with the coming winds
And danced the blues away

We sit in a circle
And that story that keeps us warm
Feeds our hearts
Makes us know

This Star city is Mine
That star at that mountain shines
For me
At me on me
Doo wap doo wap
I got the Roanoke blues
And I'm feeling fine

THE SPOTLIGHT IN THE SKY

I am the spotlight in the sky
Some call the moon

I call to the wolves to howl
With me
Sending little red riding girls
In their convertible Hondas
Home

Maybe I'm that girl everybody thinks
They know

I ride these winds
And rap with owls

The bats avoid us
Because I'm out of tune

What is this teenage thing
That we all pass through

This tunnel on the way
To grown-up-ness

Is what I see the grown-
Up world
War . . . waste . . . want

I'd rather be
In that spotlight
At break of dawn
Circling the sun
On my way to rest
Being a good Star
City called Roanoke

THE SPIDER WALTZ

A spider looked at me
And I at her
I thought a spider would be scared
      but no
She smiled and sat beside me
      in the chair
And handed me a muffin we could share

I thought "a waltz" is what this friendship needs
And so I sang a simple melody:
      Come play with me
      Come be my friend
      And I will give you butter

      Come sing a song
      And dance a waltz
      And I will give you jam

Come sing a song and dance with me
And you will be my friend
And we will laugh
And we'll have tea
And we will spin together

I WISH I COULD LIVE (IN A BOOK)

(for Charles A. Smith, Jr.)

I wish I could live
In a book
All wrapped up
In my fairy
Godmother's arms
Or sitting with my Cave
Mother baking dinosaur
Eggs

If I lived
In a book
I could fly
With Ali Baba
And even though it's not right
To steal
The Forty Thieves are
Pretty cool

Maybe there would be
A book about me
One day
Just a little girl being brave
In a world where water
Is in short supply
But everybody
Has a gun

I don't think
That's a good idea

I'd rather be in
A book
Making biscuits
On the frontier

Running with the wind
Following very lightly
On the laughter of the Prairie Dogs

That would be so nice
I think
Living in a book

I wish I could live
In music
I'd be all
Kinds:
   Opera arias
   Folk telling news
   Minuets
   Hoedown dancing
     calling square dancers
   Whoa! Bring me some
    Disco
Yeah I'd be a Spiritual
And then a wonderful
Foot-stomping Gospel tune
Some blues—almost forgot
The Blues
And we need Jazz
I need me "A-Tisket
A-Tasket"
Some little yellow basket
But not a White Horse
I'm never gonna ride
The White Horse

I want to be Little Richard
Even Donald Duck sang
   Little Richard
I mean *Quack Quack Quack Won't You Come Along*
   with Me?

Now I'm rappin'
I'm telling the news
Napster freed me
And I can choose

To have it all
For free download

Yeah I want to live
In music
Teach Learn Rejoice
In music
In music I'm free
To be a better me

There is something
About a railroad station
Not only the big pretty ones
Like in Cincinnati saying
    "Gateway to the South"
or even Boston's Back Bay with
that heroic Tina Allen sculpture of A.
    Philip Randolph
Union Station in DC . . . union being
Not only North and South
But working men and women getting
A fair wage for giving
A hard day's work
And those greatest of Black
Men . . . the Pullman Porters . . .
Who set the style . . . who took
America from primitive to privilege
Giving service all through the night
    Cooking the meals
    Setting the tables
    Washing . . . pressing so others could look
    Like gentlemen
Others sorted the mail
Which arrived
On time in the right city
No ZIP code needed thank you
These men could read
And no machine was invited
To that party

There is something about parallel
Lines moving up
And down over
Horizon and dreams never ever

97

Touching but rather on
A lonely journey with another
Lonely friend they don't talk
Though a song is sung

Parallel lines . . . not sea
Nor sky . . . hold the dreams
Of women

I wish I lived
In a painting

DON PULLEN

(for the Jefferson Center)

If dancers danced on their fingertips
Then piano players should play with their toes

The creative process is neither restrictive nor
  judgmental
It is the search for something
New and different and wonderful

Or maybe the need to make the old
Good again

It's put a stamp
On that note . . . not letter . . . and mail it
To a lonesome heart

Don Pullen sought community
Music
He wanted to play his tune
Out of tune sometimes
With friends who had another tune
To play

And if all tunes played
Their own tunes
Then wouldn't that tune be in harmony . . .
  wouldn't it?

He lived across the street
On 84th Street
From my first New York apartment

I don't play music I listen

Milford Graves, Cornell Dupree lived on that
street

Eugene McDaniels down the street
Gregory Hines around the corner and a host of
    painters and writers
Did I mention George Faison and Morgan
Freeman
And Clifton Davis came calling sometimes

What a pleasure to be
Young
And creative
And so sure of the future

We added to that conversation

And Don Pullen added to that song

MAKING A PERFECT MAN

(for Walter Leonard)

Good Morning, Ladies and Gentlemen. This morning we are going to make the perfect man.

Though you come to this enterprise with clean hands, please remember you cannot wash your hands of it. It is wise, however, to push back the wars and disease. We must understand that they are there but we will try not to wallow in them nor will we encourage any playing with them. You all remember what happened the last time we were working on men and all those hate viruses were set free. It practically took a world war to clean it up, then that Bush boy comes along shaking that blanket again.

Yes, well, the first thing to remember, Class, is that mistakes do happen. It is normal and to be expected. I always remind my students, though, to be sure to start with the best, freshest materials. I recommend the soil be flown in from Africa. There are some problems, true, but, mostly because Africa could not afford fertilizers, the soil is uncontaminated. Yes, yes, I know that sometimes the soil is sandy or weedy and a lot of times suppliers will cheat but that's why it's so important to go to reliable dealers. You pay a bit more in time and money but look at the quality.

Our task today is not the Perfect Man but The Man Perfectly suited for us.

Now, I always tell everyone, *intelligence.* I would put that in first. I know there is a school of thought that says "Intelligence can come last" or in the middle or at any time but I'm old-fashioned. If you want it, put it first. Let those other things adjust to it! I like kindly looks. I've seen enough of those pretty boys who are cruel and dumb. It may be that cruelty leads to dumbness or maybe dumbness to cruelty but either way I like a good clean sparkle in the eye.

Hold your question for a minute. I think knowing the Creator's preference helps you to know what you are expected to make. I once made seven six-foot-nine guys for the Los Angeles basketball team and I can't begin to tell you what a mistake it was. I could never smooth the arrogance out and Boy! Wow! Did we all pay for it. So I urge you on your first times to go a bit shorter. And that is also easier on Elegance. I can't begin to tell you how many times I've turned down commissions from people seeking Defensive Linesmen. There is no way to make them Elegant and I just won't be part of that. Your Quarterback, Wide Receivers . . . Yes. But the Linesmen, Offensive and Defensive . . . no way. I think football needs to go smaller anyway so that there are fewer injuries but that is not our subject this morning.

Lay out all your ingredients: good black soil, intelligence, elegance, a twinkle in each eye, and now we are getting there. Gently mix them. A lot of you young creators think you need to knock your man around but "No." Gently mix, prod, and knead. Don't forget to add ambition and once you have a good mix a pinch of ambition is the perfect elixir. Now, I prefer patience after you have let it sit and mingle with itself. Yes, yes, I know getting patience in with just the right touch can sometimes mean loneliness but that's why intelligence is so important. Remember what happened to Michael Jackson with all that talent but no balance for the loneliness which led to an overruling of intelligence and all that ugliness that followed. I think a little loneliness is not all that bad.

Some of your older creators will recommend at this point firing him up but, as I say, I'm old-fashioned. Send him off to college, grad school, ultimately let him spend some time in a northern clime with a good harbor and excellent beans. Beans are so essential to growth, both physical and emotional. What you want to do is also remember to reward him as he does the right things. I would suggest a Betty if things are going as we think. A Betty is so easy to make. A good strong piece of chocolate. I prefer chocolate for my Bettys because it's already sweet and warm. You don't have to do a lot to give it a good shape and that place in her heart can so easily be filled with both intelligence and love. In all my centuries of creating I have never had a chocolate Betty be anything less than fabulous.

It's understood that some rain will fall so send him to a small colored college in the South to help save it. Then make sure they are ungrateful. Excuse me for giggling, Class, but I just love ingratitude. In the beginning I fought so hard against ingratitude with You-Know-Who but He wouldn't listen. To shut me up He said: "Well, how can we compromise on this?" I said: "A Daughter. The only antidote to ingratitude is a daughter." I'm glad to say I was proven right on that one.

Oh, we know we've had our Adams and Georges and stuff. If this one comes out the way I think, I am planning to call him Walter: A good, strong name for a kind, elegant, intelligent, patient man. You can, at your option, add a sense of humor.

And if for some reason he's not perfect he's so close that only the perfect ones will know he's just a man. That's it for our lesson this morning.

WHEN MY PHONE TREMBLES
(for D'Angelo)

When my phone
Trembles
After midnight
I never think
   of good news:
   Someone's birthday
   An overseas friend
   Forgetting
   The time difference

I never smell
   Apples baking
   Or nutmeg dancing
   On sweet potatoes
   Yeast rolls rising
   Fish frying

I always look
   For a way to hold
   Myself
   Together
Being a '60s person
   I know
   You have to be
   Strong

When my phone trembles
After midnight
I take
A deep breath
Reach for my glasses
Think of my son

And I Pray

Please don't answer before midnight

I had a dream
Last night
I sleep with earphones to drown out fears
   Jazz mostly
   Piano jazz
With a little Milt Jackson on the side
Saying it saying it saying it clear
   "Save Your Love for Me"
But I was living in a wooded area
Very nice homes
Strange neighbors with kids and dogs and stuff
And I was in the kitchen by my mother
My father was breaking up the table
Throwing things around knocking chairs over
He didn't seem dangerous
Just mean
I picked my mother up from behind
Sort of like a heavy sack of flour
Or birdseed or even gravel for the pond
And carried her out
Then when I sat her down we were back in the
   kitchen again

I took her to a vehicle
I want to say a "car" but it wasn't a car
No no don't answer until midnight I won't be
   ready until then
And I drove away
It was as curvy as all get-out—a dirt road that was
Actually a lovely brown
But when we stopped we were back
In the kitchen

My sister was looking
And I was trying to say something
Which came out all crazy
So this 2 is not a poem
Because if it were a poem
I would put my head in your lap
And cry and cry
But since it is not a poem it must be
A painting *Still Life with Crying Girl*
And what we would see is a bowl of half-eaten
   raspberries
Mint leaves drenched in the sugary liquid
And a little fly
Poised in the corner
At midnight attracted by the fly
The common vampire bat
On the light of a moonbeam
Will come to hold my head

ROBERT CHAMPION

(Who Died at the Hands of His Bandmates)

The ever restless ocean
Beating against sea
And sky
Grinds, no gently rubs,
The bones of Robert Champion
Into the salt
Of his ancestors
Driven into the blue
Through Middle Passage

We know the torture
Of slavery
And apartheid
We know the terror
Of Jim Crow
Who would imagine The Band
Would kill

Are we having too many
Black men trying to sing
A praise song
Too many Black men trying
To show a better self
So many Black men
That we can spare them

I don't think so

There can be no excuse
For this murder
There can be no I didn't
Realize he was dying
How could you not know

When you act like nazis
Jesus is crucified

How could you not understand

This child should have lived

How could Black men do this
to each other?

I killed a spider
Not a murderous brown recluse
Nor even a black widow
And if the truth were told this
Was only a small
Sort of papery spider
Who should have run
When I picked up the book
But she didn't
And she scared me
And I smashed her

I don't think
I'm allowed

To kill something

Because I am

Frightened

FLYING IN KIGALI

Or

War Is Never Right

For some reason
Or perhaps
None
The dew was just lifting
Which is not unreasonable
But something for no reason
Made me walk
In my house slippers
To the little dogwood tree
Recently planted
By the shed

As I watered the tree
And, frankly, took joy
In the grass coming up
Where I had tried
For several years to no avail
To grow this little spot of green
I spotted a furry thing

Without thinking
I turned the hose on it
Assuming it was a mushroom
Or some of the mold
That occasionally forms
On top of the mulch

I know there could not
Have been a scream because
Screams aren't possible
For little birds
But there was a protest

My heart broke
This little robin was out of the nest
Before she could fly
And I live with a Yorkie
Who was sniffing the yard

I grabbed the dog
Taking her back inside
And returned
To understand
This little bird would die

The mother was overhead now
And I put the bird in a basket
To take her beyond the reach
Of Alex though surely
Into the paw
Of one of the cats that roam

Some will say: *It's Mother Nature's
way* Some will say: *It's Natural*
Some will say: *It is out of your hands
There is* Nothing *you can do about it*

But it still breaks my heart
To know that little robin
Cannot be saved

TEREZIN: WHERE THIRTY-FIVE THOUSAND DIED
BUT IT WAS NOT A DEATH CAMP

I don't want you
To watch me sleeping I don't want you
To look worriedly
Over me
In some hospital bed
Tied up with tubes
Laboring over my breath
Until I take that last one
And release my energy

There was a deer
In the middle of Highway 81
She had been hit
And could not run
While waiting for some uninterested trucker
She held up her head

And I
In cowardly concern
Turned away

There was
On a cold snowy night
Coming across the West Virginia Turnpike
A rabbit which tried to cross
Four lanes of traffic
The head was hit
But hadn't yet told the legs
So they kept running

And I from fatigue
And helplessness drove
On

Slavery was not fun
The holocaust happened
People are not good
And yet we go on

Until we stop

And I think
The only bravery available
To us
Is to Remember

Smell—
As we all know—
Is half the taste

TO THE LION WHO DISCOVERED A DEER IN HIS HABITAT: GIVE HIM KETCHUP!

Because who was knocking on my door
After midnight

I know it wasn't you
'Cause you said:
This is it. I am out of here. I don't want to hear it
  anymore

And I said:
Well go. You think I care?

Ergo I know it wasn't you
Needing my arms
Or my kisses
Not to mention my roast beef

So who was knocking at that hour

Last night night before
24 robbers at my door
I got up let them in
Hit them in the head
With a rolling pin
All hid?

And the lion pounced
Because it was such a treat
The chance to butcher his own meat

Not that the zoo butcher didn't cut a fine roast
But hell
He could for the first time in his life
Do it himself

Remember when you were learning to walk
And your mom would hold your hand

Remember when you started dressing yourself
And your big sister laughed at your stripes and
    plaids
Well that lion didn't have anyone to answer to
    now
But himself

Imagine his pride when he carted dinner home
That night
Imagine the good good love they would make
While she crooned what a lion he is

And then the zookeeper came and said:
Deer is not good for you

Yes, dear, she said, *I am*

Pass the ketchup, Mr. Zookeeper
You or the antelope?

Fresher Meat, Better Tasting
Papa John

THE SIGNIFICANCE OF POETRY

Poetry is as necessary
To life
As salt is to stew
As garlic is to pasta
As perfume is to summer nights
As shaving lotion is to mornings
As your smile is to
My happiness

Poetry is as significant
To life
As yeast is to bread
As butter is to toast
As grapes are to wine
As sugar is to lemons
How else will we get
Lemonade

Poetry is to me
Your voice
Your touch
Your laughter
That feeling at the end of day
That I am
Not alone

NOTE TO THE SOUTH: YOU LOST

The buzz of the flies
Almost was a lullaby
Rocking the dead
To a restful place

You couldn't hear the ants
Though they were
Clearly there
In the eyes the mouths
Any wound or soft
Tissue

The worms had come
Understanding those
Which were not
Trampled
Would have a great
Feast

The grasses had no
Choice but to drink
Down the blood
And bits of flesh
That were ground
Into them

In the future
It would be girls
Not field rats
Who would follow
The soldiers
Into the trenches

In the future there
Would be single
Engine airplanes
Dropping bombs

And then
In the scientific imagination
Of the 21st century
There would be men

And women
Pushing buttons
Making war clean
And distant

But today
On This battlefield
The deadliest of This war
The Songbirds had been
Frightened off

The Turkey Buzzards retreated to watch
Deer Skunk Raccoons
Possum Groundhogs gathered
To let the smoke clear

And only the moans
Of the almost dead
And the quiet march of Lice
Gave cadence to this concert of sacrifice
For
Freedom

THE GOLDEN SHOVEL POEM

they eat beans mostly, this old yellow pair
—From "The Bean Eaters" by Gwendolyn Brooks

At the Evening of Life

I wonder if **they**
See the evening of life as a treat to **eat**
Or as a staple like **beans**
With corn bread **mostly**
A good warming meal **this**
Daily day **old**
Bread pudding love capped sunshine **yellow**
By an honest upstanding **pair**

Pinto Beans Fried Corn Bread
Clean Spring Water Rocking Chair
Your Smile Home Peace

FOR SONIA SANCHEZ

In the name of those incredibly Brave men and
   women
who made the Trek from Freedom in Africa to
   Enslavement in America
and maintained their humanity
through unspeakable acts

In the precious name of Phillis Wheatley
who was put on Academic Trial
forcing her to prove she wrote her own Poems

to the confident Paul Laurence Dunbar
who kept the plantation tongue alive

In the Brave name of W. E. B. DuBois
who studied The Atlantic Slave Trade

to Jessie Fauset
who wrote children's stories

In the name of the incomparable Langston
Hughes
who taught us
The tom-tom cries and
the tom-tom laughs

to the anger of Richard Wright

In the name of the Honesty of James Baldwin
In the fearlessness of Margaret Walker
to the beautiful poems of Gwendolyn Brooks

In the name of the awesome Toni Morrison
And the truly wonderful spirit of Rita Dove

In the names of those whom we silently call
and in the names of those whose names will call us
in the future

This is for
Sonia Sanchez

Words are the lifeblood of writers. Though I must admit I don't know if we dream in words or if we word our dreams.

Words are like quilts. You have to put a bunch together to make something warm and comforting or patch together something that will prick and scratch the spirit. No matter how we weave this experience, we sculpt an idea and shape a phrase.

A phrase. Usually we find phrases to describe whatever it is. No word is sufficient to stand alone. Not even strong words like FREEDOM or soft words like LOVE. They all are better when added to . . . for example FOR ALL . . . or *Je t'aime*. Love phrases work in all languages.

The human experiment has turned on many important phrases WE THE PEOPLE, **taxation without representation** and even things like REMEMBER THE MAINE. There are other political phrases like LIBERTÉ, ÉGALITÉ, FRATERNITÉ. I especially like WE SHALL OVERCOME. There are personal phrases like **Yes**. Which may be the only one-word phrase we ever use. **No** requires a bit more. There are personal phrases such as **You Look Beautiful** and **I am so proud of you** but maybe that's a sentence not a phrase.

The human imagination is the engine that has carried us from caves in Europe, from the rain forests of South America, from the lush and mineral-rich lands of Africa, from the beautiful amber waves of North America, from the roaring seas and the frozen tundra to this meeting with these artists here at Virginia Tech and, in fact, to wherever humans gather.

There are philosophical phrases, theological phrases, scientific phrases, economic phrases, political phrases, phrases to explain and express. BUT there is one phrase that, if a phrase could be said to jump-start the human heart, we all know and love. Writers took up this phrase from the griots and soothsayers of old. As we began this journey with words, which is yet ever expanding our emotional and physical universe, we still find in our darkest hours and our most joyful moments the need to gather 'round the fire, or circle the wagons, or tuck into bed the young and the old with the enchantment of that magical phrase "Once Upon A Time . . . " We know the storyteller has arrived. We comfort our spirits to think and dream. We know those other magical words will follow: In A Land Far Away . . . and our imaginations can soar safe within the hopes and sometimes the prayers.

I have written the essay below to help explain how I edit my poetry. I am more inclined to say I create a path through which I hope to take the reader rather than finding a perfect word to make the reader follow my thought. I have chosen a new poem: **COFFEE** because I actually did make a new pathway once I gave it a second or third look. I think the second version is an easier walk. I wrote to share my feelings about the edit.

Job (Y)

(Y)our Job Safety Is Our Priority: A Path for Poetry

(should read "our job safety is your priority"
but I cannot make my computer cross things out)

A poem is not so much read as navigated. We go from point to point discovering a new horizon, a shift of light or laughter, an exhilaration of newness that we had missed before. Even familiar, or perhaps especially familiar, poems bring the excitement of first nighters, first encounters, first love . . . when viewed and reviewed.

I'm not a big fan of adjust this line, change this word, add a *this* subtract a *that*. The poem like the kitten, like the tadpole, like the moth *is* and with time will mature to *become*. Sometimes it gets consumed to make another poem better—sometimes it simply is out in the world too long and dries up—sometimes a friendly scout seeing the struggle of the butterfly to break free from the cocoon decides to make the struggle easier and cuts her loose . . . call it an MFA program workshopping a poem too much. She falls to the ground, unable to soar because a doer of good deeds didn't want to see the pain. Though now all that is left is a tenure-track position and the bitterness of tears shed for dreams not unwon but unchased.

I like to think poems are maps—they don't Google but rather guide us along the way. There is no destination on a country road. You see an old woman slightly bent moving through the field. A frisky calf frolicking. Sometimes a deer standing still. Why would there be a destination when life itself is a journey? You go not to get there but to be there.

On my good days I like to think a glass of *blanc de blanc* (as real champagne is for movie stars and presidents), a bit of sun through the clouds, my backyard birds singing, the koi contentedly lazing through the pool, and Alex, my little Yorkie friend, and I are a country road. We meander, we laugh, we would like to love. We are a journey—a poem. Open us. Explore. Inhale. Wonder.

COFFEE (original)

Vitamin C prevents
Colds
A and D do sunshine
Things
We need calcium
For strong bones
There must be something
For the eyes
Carrots, Cabbage, Lettuce
You never saw
A blind rabbit
And I have a friend
Who thinks Salmon
Will prevent
A loss of your mind
But I believe
In Coffee
    Drip
    Percolated
    Pressed
    Coffee

Black not sweet
No cream
Coffee
Which smells like morning
And feels like friendship
Coffee
While we laugh
And preview
Our day

COFFEE (edited)

Vitamin C prevents
Colds

A and D do sunshine
Things

We need Calcium
For strong bones
And

There must be something
For the eyes
    Carrots, Cabbage, Lettuce
You never saw
A blind rabbit

And I have a friend
Who thinks Salmon
Will prevent
A loss of your mind

But I believe
In Coffee
   Drip
   Percolated
   Pressed
   Coffee
Black not sweet
No cream
Coffee
Which smells like morning
And feels like friendship

Coffee

While we laugh
And preview
Our day

The Journey: The journey begins with the idea. It begins with a story. The journey is the step any writer takes to declare: I have something to say. I have a voice. I need to Use it. Since poetry is my vehicle on this journey, I chose to form my own publishing company and publish myself. I learned to set type, to bind, to cut. These skills are not necessary in the computer age, but they were then. Skills give us freedom. Freedom gives us wings.

The Inspiration: I am a lover of history. It was Malcolm X who said: "Of all our endeavors, history is the most qualified to reward all research." That may not be a totally accurate quote, but I remember being enchanted with heroes, with quests, with the search for the difficult and the unknown. Human beings are worthy of our interest. I continue to be fascinated by who we are and of which greatness we are capable.

The Back Story: My latest book, *Bicycles,* evolved out of personal and professional sadness. A murder in the city in which I live and a massacre at the university at which I work formed the anchors of the book. But anchors are stationary and these two events kept spinning. It occurred to me that they were wheels. If that was the case then how could I connect them? Tragedy can only be calmed by love and laughter; I challenged myself to write love poems to connect the vents to the energy that was spinning. Once that journey was started, I realized if I put a handle on it I would have a Bicycle; hence my title. Love requires trust and balance. A perfect description of a bike.

The Buzz: It is a pleasure to report *Bicycles* was well received.

The State of the Industry: My very latest book is an anthology: *The 100* Best African American Poems (*but I cheated).* I cheated because I wanted to put more than just the 100 historical poems. That would take me from Phillis Wheatley to the Black

Arts movement and maybe, if I pushed it, to Tupac, but I felt my obligation was to do more. So we numbered the book 1 to 100 but we stuffed poems into duets, and suites, communities, even. The book has 221 poems in all and I am very proud of that. I believe our job as both writers and editors is to keep pushing the envelope.

There has never been a time when human beings did not create art. We tend to say the Caveman painted the walls but that would be illogical: He was out either hunting or protecting the front of the cave. Cave woman drew on those walls to leave a record—some . . . one . . . was here. We began with the Egyptians to see representations of humans and to see drawings that could easily be explained as prayers for a benign God.

People have also always sung . . . made noises that were either warning of danger or offering courtship. There will always be a need for song.

But there will also always be a need for physical representation. For paintings, now photographs, soon only digital and maybe something else yet unknown but not so far away.

Football is art. Almost a ballet. Reaching for the ball twirling down. Sprinting for the goal. Basketball is an art. Taking off mid-court and flying for a dunk. Black men made an art of walking. That thrust of hips, that *gangsta* lean. Folk saw that and wanted to throw their cars away.

Black people *are* a work of art. In the deepest throes of slavery we found a tone to build upon that became The Negro Spiritual. They laughed. Nobody, they said, wanted to hear it. But we sang on. Sang to Gospel to make it jazz to make it rhythm and blues to have it stolen as *rock* to make it Rap. The only sound, besides jazz, that is heard all over this planet. Black Americans are wonderful. They laughed at Duke Ellington: called it Jungle Music. They said Marian Anderson couldn't sing in the DAR building so she sang to the Heavens. They laughed at our poetry: said it was angry. They laughed at Rap: said it was dangerous.

They don't know what to make of the representational art today. It can be called Graffiti which in some eyes diminishes that art. No matter what they call it today, tomorrow they will call it **Genius**. Tomorrow they will teach classes about it; write books about it; give lectures on it. Folk will be awarded tenure for explaining why this line goes that way though of course only you and I know why. The artist felt it. The artist was true to herself; true to himself.

There would be those who say you cannot do what you do; you need to please the masses. But for those of us outside The Magic Circle, the masses we serve, our ancestors, our communities, our prayers for a fairer future . . . we are pleasing. Good for us. Good for everybody who has stayed true to ourselves.

Hip Hop Lives. And this art will live on as a testament to the beginning of the 21st Century. Alain Locke was correct when he said The Harlem Renaissance would define a great people because no people are great without great art. We are a great people.

I give
easily
because I have
easily
taken It's incredibly
difficult
to let people
give you what you need maybe
as difficult as
giving you what you want
interactions
with and between
humans can certainly be
complicated

People who live alone
Fart in cars
Pick their noses
Sleep naked
And never flush
In the middle of the night

Most people who live alone
Are compulsive
Things have to stay where
Things were put
People too
Like there is no room
In my heart for change
Or hamburger that I don't grind
Or coffee that drips
Or tears because
People who live alone
Soon learn
It is all
right

BEFORE YOU JUMP OFF A BRIDGE OR HANG YOURSELF OR
BE UNHAPPY PLEASE CONSIDER: LIVE FOR YOURSELF;
THOSE WHO HATE YOU HAVE NO PURCHASE

I don't think
There is

a   definition

        or

b   definition

        but only

the   definition
when it comes to who you R

but then I don't
Facebook   or
Twitter   or
YouTube   or
Ask anyone's permission

To fuck or not to fuck
That is not the question

To love or to be
Lonely:
No-brainer

Who you are
Is you
And no one can

Should
Or
Will
Touch
that

YOU GAVE HER SOMETHING
(for Big Nikky)

You said: My aunt owned
A building where she rented
Apartments
Like Macon Dead's tenants sometimes
They couldn't pay
Twice over the years the man
Upstairs gave paintings
Instead of money

He said: Will you take this
Will you take that
For my staying in
Your place here on earth

And she said: Yes

You said: I visited and loved
Them both
My aunt told me the story of the paintings

They are extraordinary, I said to her

She said: Take them. I want you to have them

You carried these paintings
From coast to coast South to less South
To the walls of a warm and comforting home

You said to me: Do you know the painter
Do you know what they are now worth
If I had known their worth I would have
Should have given her something
For them

I said: You Did
You love her You love the paintings
If that's not something
Then I know nothing

THIRST

At 2:30 or maybe 3:00 A.M. I have tossed
And turned all I can:
I'm thirsty

But if I get up to drink I'll have to
Get up again
To go to the bathroom

Thirst wins

Stumbling into my house
Shoes
I go to the kitchen
To find the lemonade

My mother
Were she still here
Would complain:
You don't drink enough water.
Adam's Ale is the best thing
But I don't like water
I, like most Americans,
Take my water
With sugar or fruit juices
Or any disguise I can find

Leaning over the sink
With a bit of real lemonade dripping down
My chin
I feel the coolness
Float into my lungs
And that blessed relief
That says Thirst
Has been satisfied

Feeling myself once again in bloom
I smile
Return to my bed
And await my next
          Adventure.

On a foggy night
With that sort of misty rain
That is wonderful for sleeping
But nothing at all for driving
I traveled home
From a great dinner party

We were all so jolly

Driving my ninety-year-old aunt
Who was visiting from out of town
We were catching up on family

And arguing politics

I turned up our mountain
Just as I admonished her:
But The President hasn't done anything
About jobs
When something said:
    You are going too fast

It may have been the wine that evening
But I have to confess:
I speed a lot

So I heeded the voice

My eyes always sweep the Trail
Leading to my home

From Side to Side

There is always a cat
Or raccoon seldom a coyote and at this hour of
night the turtles
And snakes are in bed

My aunt asked: *Why*
Are you hitting your brakes

When a beautiful white strip
Surrounded by shiny black fur
With fear in her eyes
Got caught in my headlights
And stopped

I stopped too

And waited.

She continued her journey across the trail
And I hope
Home to her babies

We need to watch
For the scared and the vulnerable

One day it may be
Us

The author gratefully acknowledges the following publications in which poems in *Chasing Utopia* first appeared, sometimes in slightly different form:

"Chasing Utopia": *Poetry Magazine*

"Spices," "The International Open," and "It's Just Love": *Appalachian Heritage*

"Icarus": *Icarus: The Wyoming High School Magazine*

"When God Made Mountains": *The Knoxville Journal*

"These Women": *Tiferet Journal*

"Poets": *Cultural Weekly*

"In Defense of Flowers": *The Roanoke Times*

"Exercise": *Cerise Press*

"I Wish I Could Live (in a Book)": *What You Wish For: A Book for Darfur*

"Don Pullen": *The Jefferson Center Tribute to Don Pullen*

"When My Phone Trembles" and "The Scared and the Vulnerable": *Prairie Schooner*

"Note to the South: You Lost," previously published as "The Lost Cause Lost": *Lines in a Long Array: A Civil War Commemoration: Poems and Photographs, Past and Present*

"Our Job Safety Is Your Priority with Coffee": *The Atlantic*

NIKKI GIOVANNI, poet, activist, mother, and professor, is a seven-time NAACP Image Award winner and the first recipient of the Rosa Parks Woman of Courage Award, and holds the Langston Hughes Medal for Outstanding Poetry, among many other honors. The author of twenty-eight books and a Grammy nominee for *The Nikki Giovanni Poetry Collection,* she is the University Distinguished Professor of English at Virginia Tech in Blacksburg, Virginia.